RIGHTS VERSUS ANTITRUST

RIGHTS VERSUS ANTITRUST

Challenging the Ethics of Competition Law

Mark D. White

agenda
publishing

First published in 2024 by Agenda Publishing

Agenda Publishing Limited
PO Box 185
Newcastle upon Tyne
NE20 2DH

www.agendapub.com

ISBN 978-1-78821-433-9 (hardcover)
ISBN 978-1-78821-715-6 (paperback)

British Library Cataloguing-in-Publication Data
A catalogue record for this book is available
from the British Library

Typeset in Nocturne by Patty Rennie

Printed and bound by CPI Group (UK) Ltd, Croydon, CR0 4YY

Contents

Preface

> The right to swing my fist ends where your nose begins.
>
> (Common aphorism)

In liberal democracies, we are accustomed to a wide range and degree of freedom, limited only by the equally valid freedom of others. In other words, individuals are presumed to have the right to pursue their interests, whatever they may be, provided they do not wrongfully interfere with others doing the same.

The word "wrongfully" is crucial here. The five people ahead of me in the line for coffee in the morning are definitely interfering with my interests, but they are not acting wrongfully if they simply arrived there before I did. However, if someone arrives after me and cuts in front of me, that person is acting wrongfully, violating an important social norm, even if not a legal one. If I manage to procure my treasured beverage and then, upon leaving the coffee shop, someone attacks me and steals my coffee, that person has violated a clear legal norm, and I can marshal the powers of the state to my side to pursue justice. (My sole recourse to the person who cut in line is to express scorn and hope my fellow patrons do the same.)

Although we may resent those who have a negative impact on our lives, we should also recognize when they had every right to their actions. Each of us interacts with countless other people in myriad ways every day, inevitably leading to blameless conflict, due only to scarcity of time and space (and coffee shops). It is only when people violate social or legal norms, implying rights held by others, do those actions become wrongful—and it is only when actions are wrongful that we feel justified in addressing them in some way, whether by scorn (in the case of social norms) or state action (in the case of legal norms).

This idea applies not only to individual actions, but to those of businesses as well. Firms take many actions that affect individuals (and other firms) in positive and negative ways, but even the latter is not of concern to the state unless they violate recognized rights. Businesses can increase prices, stop producing certain products, or close locations, all of them possibly setting back the interests of individuals who enjoyed or relied on them. And these are just their activities that affect consumers: firms also take many actions with respect to employees, creditors, and other businesses they work with, all of which have effects on those other parties, for better or for worse.

Even though businesses can cause harm with all of these activities, we recognize that they have wide latitude to conduct their affairs as long as they do not violate the rights of their consumers, employees, creditors, or trading partners. We can complain when the price of coffee increases, or our local shop no longer carries our favorite roast, or shuts down completely, but we have no legal recourse to prevent these actions. The same goes for the shop's employees, creditors, and suppliers, all of whom have the same rights to change their behavior (as do their customers), but not to interfere with those of the coffee shop. Only when the business violates rights, such as by deceptive or coercive practices, does it behave wrongfully, which can and should be addressed through the legal system.

This is what I regard as the commercial ideal in a liberal democracy: businesses and consumers (and other related parties) freely acting and interacting within constraints provided by the rights of all, with violations of these rights punished under the law. For the most part, this is the picture of commerce those of living in liberal democracies see around us. Of course, there are limitations on business in the form of regulations that govern treatment of workers, product safety, and environmental practices, which can all be formulated in the language of rights protection. Each of these is controversial, as most laws are, but they can be justified in terms of the recognized rights and protected interests of those affected, and therefore are valid interferences with the free interaction of business with their consumers, employees, and other partners.

And then we have antitrust.

I shall argue in this book that, despite the wide consensus among academics, policymakers, and elected leaders across the political spectrum, the legal institution of antitrust is anathema to liberal democracy. Antitrust betrays our most basic understandings of property rights and economic liberty—not just those of libertarians or classic liberals, but those of the majority of people living in liberal democracies with market economies, ranging from Sweden to Singapore, with the United States somewhere in the middle. Antitrust sacrifices the rights of some for the well-being of others by neglecting what rights are actually meant to do. It punishes firms, not for doing wrong, but for not doing enough good. It implies that business exists, not to express the interests and agency of individuals, but as mere means to promoting economic welfare—or, in more political orientations of antitrust, democracy itself. In other words, antitrust holds businesses responsible for a role they have no obligation to fulfill, which represents a grave misunderstanding of the nature of commerce in a free society.

If you're not inclined to be sympathetic to the titans of industry, consider if the same obligations were imposed on you as a consumer or employee. Imagine that your choices regarding what goods and services to buy, where to shop, and what career you could pursue and for whom, were permitted only insofar as they served the interests of the state or society as a whole. If you happened to make choices that coincided with the greater good, you would never encounter any interference. But if you decided to buy beef when buying chicken would do more for the economy, or chose to be a writer (*gasp*) when working as an engineer is declared to be of more value, then your preferred choices would be foreclosed. You would be obligated to make choices that served the greater good, as opposed to the liberal tradition of a zone of autonomy in which you can make your choices regarding your own life, provided (once again) that your actions do not infringe on the same rights of others.

But we are not accorded this same consideration when acting commercially as businesses. In countries with antitrust or competition law—which is to say most industrialized countries—business firms are prevented from taking actions that are seen as counterproductive to broader economic well-being. This goes against the understanding of business in liberal societies as the free expression of individuals' interests. In a market economy, some persons sell their labor (by working), some their capital (by investing), and some exercise their entrepreneurial drive through starting or joining businesses. There is no obvious reason why, when people choose the third option, their options are limited by their potential to increase societal well-being, or why they should face more scrutiny than workers or investors (provided that they are doing nothing wrongful).

In writing this book, I have tried to keep my argument as straightforward and lighthearted as I can, in hopes of inspiring readers from a variety of backgrounds to reconsider the wisdom of antitrust and competition law. To that end, I do not get into the fine details of antitrust statutes, judicial opinions, or legal cases, or the various interpretations or implementations of these laws around the globe. All I rely on are some concepts from economics, philosophy, and law, which I explain fully before applying them to the general idea of antitrust—and, most important, the basic and common belief that individuals should be free to pursue their own interests provided they do not wrongfully interfere with others doing the same.

Acknowledgements

The road to this book has been a long one, starting with a letter to the editor published in *The Wall Street Journal* on 2 April 2003, brashly proclaiming antitrust to be "anathema" to a free market system. Over 20 years and two journal articles later, a book has finally emerged. I've long called this book my "white whale," but I finally "caught" it—now let's see where it takes me.

I thank Alison Howson, Steven Gerrard, and the team at Agenda, who gave me the opportunity to write this book the way I always wanted to write it, and two anonymous referees, who understood the way I wrote it and showed me how to make it better.

I thank Ed Stringham, who published my first antitrust paper in the *Journal of Private Enterprise Education* after I presented it at the Association for Private Enterprise Education meetings at the Southern Economic Association conference, and the Intercollegiate Studies Institute, who later honored me with the Templeton Enterprise Award for it.

I thank Raju Parakkal, who accepted my second antitrust paper into his symposium on "Capitalism, Antitrust, and Democracy," and Bill Curran, who published it (with critical replies from Ryan Long and Alan Barr) in the *Antitrust Bulletin*.

I thank Richard Epstein, who has long been an inspiration and an advocate.

Finally, I thank Dominick Armentano, who in my opinion said the first and last word on the problems with antitrust, and with whom I was honored to share that *Wall Street Journal* letters column over 20 years ago.

1

Overview

In arguing against the entire field of antitrust and competition law, I have set myself quite the task. After all, antitrust is a largely unquestioned part of law and regulation in most developed countries around the world. In the United States, antitrust law has been raised to a level of importance normally reserved for the seminal documents of liberal democracy itself. For example, in 1972 the Supreme Court pronounced that

> Antitrust laws in general, and the Sherman Act in particular, are the Magna Carta of free enterprise. They are as important to the preservation of economic freedom and our free enterprise system as the Bill of Rights is to the protection of our fundamental personal freedoms. And the freedom guaranteed each and every business, no matter how small, is the freedom to compete—to assert with vigor, imagination, devotion, and ingenuity whatever economic muscle it can muster.[1]

Earlier, the Court called the Sherman Act "a comprehensive charter of economic liberty aimed at preserving free and unfettered competition as the rule of trade."[2] Indeed, according to political scientist Marc Allen Eisner, "antitrust was often referred to as a constitution for the American economy," reflecting the centrality it has come to occupy in the firmament of economic regulation.[3]

Although liberals and conservatives maintain their own unique focus and emphasis for antitrust, most scholars and policymakers across the political spectrum support some degree of antitrust enforcement. As economists Kenneth Elzinga and William Breit wrote, antitrust is "one of those rare issues that cuts across even the most formidable of ideological barriers."[4] Democratic U.S. Senator Howard Metzenbaum, writing in the *Antitrust Law Journal* in 1987, asserted that "if you are for free enterprise, then you must be for antitrust. You can't be for one and against the other."[5] By the same token, economist George Stigler of the University of Chicago—a school famous for a restrained approach to competition law—claimed that antitrust is "public interest law in the same sense in which . . . having private property, enforcement of contracts, and suppression of crime are public-interest phenomena."[6]

Regardless of the approach taken to antitrust—whether traditional, structuralist, Chicago, Harvard, post-Chicago, or Neo-Brandeisian—most all scholars and policymakers today agree that antitrust is an essential aspect of the legal system regulating the economy. It is rarely questioned at a fundamental level, but instead taken for granted, having become, in Eisner's words, "as much a national tradition as an economy-wide microeconomic policy."[7] Economist Andrew Shonfield went so far as to claim that "it is best understood when it is treated as a form of national religion," a comment that can be easily written off as hyperbole if not for the uncritical nature in which it is accepted by the academy, the government, and the public as a whole.[8]

THE GOALS OF ANTITRUST

Although there is general agreement on the "if" question, there is more debate regarding the "how." One of the perennial debates in the antitrust literature, involving both academics and practitioners, deals with the appropriate focus, orientation, and goals of antitrust itself, with a primary axis of disagreement being the proper role of economics in antitrust enforcement.[9]

It is widely accepted that the original antitrust statutes in the United States, the Sherman and Clayton Acts, were motivated more by political or populist concerns—protecting the "little guy," including consumers and competitors, against concentrated business power—than economic in any modern, theoretical sense. Legal scholar Richard Posner describes this orientation toward antitrust as being "based on a hostility toward wealth and power and a suspicion of capitalism but a suspicion that falls short of an endorsement of socialism."[10] Those legislators' worries were focused on "bigness," as law professor Tim Wu calls it, representing the state's fear of the growing power of business rivaling its own—a democratic concern, as much as the generally economic one of protecting small competitors from large ones.[11]

Power, a dominant theme in the early debates over antitrust, has been revived of late. Advocates such as Wu and law professor Lina Khan—who both worked for the Biden administration, Wu as Special Assistant to the President for Technology and Competition Policy and Khan as chairperson of the Federal Trade Commission—have advocated forcefully for a return to the pro-democracy and anti-bigness purpose of the original antitrust legislation, as well as the jurisprudence of U.S. Supreme Court Justice Louis Brandeis (giving this new movement the title of "Neo-Brandeisian").[12] Due to this populist approach, antitrust has enjoyed renewed attention in recent years, including a book by U.S. Senator (and one-time presidential candidate) Amy Klobuchar, who champions the work of Khan, Wu, and other progressive antitrust advocates.[13]

Nonetheless, the dominant orientation of antitrust for over half a century has been economic, specifically in the sense of the microeconomic theory of the firm, markets, and the law. Naturally, economics has always played some role in the justification of antitrust: even in the early years, it was clear that concentration of economic power led to negative outcomes for consumers and small competitors, without relying on technical economic theory to measure or quantify it. This intuitive style of economics became more formalized with the "structure-conduct-performance" school of thinking that dominated academic studies of industrial organization in the mid-twentieth century, which held that a more concentrated industry led to more restrained behavior on the part of firms, and thereby to higher prices and lower output for consumers.[14]

3

As the field of industrial organization became more technically rigorous in the 1970s, economists dismissed the informal structure-conduct-performance paradigm and replaced it with mathematical analysis and game theory. Following suit, many antitrust scholars and authorities refined their own economic approach based on market theory, welfare economics, and cost–benefit analysis. The standard-bearer for a microeconomics-based approach to competition and anti-trust was the Chicago School of Economics and its associated "Chicago approach" to antitrust, as reflected by Robert Bork's landmark 1978 book *The Antitrust Paradox*.[15] Among the broad range of issues Bork addresses, the most influential contribution is his forceful argument for a consumer welfare standard for antitrust enforcement, in which firms would be investigated and prosecuted only for collusive actions that resulted in harm to consumers through higher prices, regardless of the effect on concentration itself.[16] He was also skeptical of any sig-nificant long-term negative effects from predatory pricing, in which dominant firms lower prices, not to attract customers but allegedly to drive out less efficient competitors so they can raise prices afterwards. Other schools of antitrust, such as Harvard and post-Chicago, take dif-ferent approaches to the nature of competition and the importance of strategic behavior, but for the most part they share the Chicago school's concern with consumer well-being, which has since come to dominate antitrust thinking in both academia and policy (with exceptions noted above).[17]

Although my argument in this book will focus primarily on the dominant economic orientation of antitrust, it also applies to the more explicitly political or populist issues of concentrated corporate power, "bigness," and concerns for democracy that characterize the Neo-Brandeisian movement. From the perspective I present here, the economic and political orientations for antitrust, although diametri-cally opposed in the eyes of their respective advocates, suffer from the same problem: both see firms as means to a societal end rather than as expressions of individual autonomy (or ends in themselves). In both views, business owners are expected to subordinate their own interests and goals to those of society as a whole, and are held responsible for the failure of those societal goals, regardless of any grounds for moral obligation toward them.

RIGHT, WRONGS, AND HARMS

One essential idea that is missing from most of the discussion of antitrust is the concept of rights, whether held by business owners or consumers. We shall explore the complex nature of rights more in the pages that follow, but for now suffice it to say that antitrust advocates rarely invoke *any* rights violated by firms that would justify constraints on their activity.[18] Insofar as it is driven by economic theory—which itself does not recognize any meaningful concept of rights—antitrust requires businesses to abstain from practices that would lessen their contribution to total economic welfare or consumer well-being, an obligation that no other private participant in the economy shares. As we shall see, antitrust relies on a crude application of a questionable moral philosophy to allow the state to challenge any business activity that it feels does not serve the interests of the economy as a whole—or, more often, simply the consumers within it. Furthermore, these limitations on the rights of businesses are imposed with no justification in the form of any recognized rights on the part of consumers. In the understanding of antitrust enforcers, any action of business owners is subject to the review by the state if it is suspected they might not advance broader economic interests.

When we examine antitrust through the lens of rights, we see that it constrains the rights of business owners to dispense with their property—the goods and services they sell, or even the business itself—with no justification based on a violation of the rights of anyone else, including consumers. As I shall argue, consumers have no established or recognized right to a certain economic outcome, such as low prices, that would counterbalance firms' right to set high ones (which is not even a legal issue unless this right is exercised in conjunction with other firms). No consumer has a right to a certain minimum number of firms in an industry that would justify constraining mergers.

If we instead look at competitors as the victims of anticompetitive

5

behavior, we find that, unlike consumers, they are often harmed by low prices, both in the short term (in the form of lower profits) and the long term (if sustained low prices drive less efficient firms from the industry). But competitors, regardless of how efficient they are, also have no rights to a certain market environment—and to the extent antitrust encourages more intense competition to benefit consumers and maintain low prices, inhibiting it to protect the hypothetical rights of inefficient firms defeats its purpose.

To be sure, firm behavior that violates antitrust law often results in harm to consumers. As callous as it may sound, however, consumers have no right to be free from that harm. If a business shuts down or moves away, its customers may be harmed, but no one would question the right of the firm to close or move. If a business unilaterally raises its prices, its customers may be harmed, but again, no one would question the right of the firm to raise its price. Consumers are harmed in both cases, which is unfortunate, but they have no specific right *not* to be. Because no right is violated, these examples of business behavior are not wrongful; rather, they are legitimate business actions to further the owners' interests.

My argument is that nothing changes when we look at firm behavior in violation of antitrust. Consumers have no rights that protect them against one firm merging assets with another firm, firms using exclusionary practices to impair the performance of other firms, and even coordinating with other firms to fix prices. These are not wrongful actions in the sense that they violate rights; rather, they are valid exercises of the business owners' property rights. Those familiar with antitrust may answer that these actions are wrong because they are prohibited by law, but I am arguing against that prohibition itself, because there is no basis for it from the viewpoint of rights. These actions are illegal for the simple reason that they serve to lower total welfare and raise consumer prices, which I am arguing is an insufficient basis for criminalizing business conduct.

ECONOMICS IS NOT JUST ECONOMICS

Although I engage in this book mostly with the economic orientation to antitrust, I take no issue with the economic analysis itself. What I do take issue with is how that economic analysis is framed, understood, and used to justify the prohibition of legitimate business activity.

One of the most widespread misconceptions that I shall argue against is that antitrust is "purely an economic matter." For example, Richard Posner, a key figure in the economic approach to law (as well as a former U.S. federal appellate judge), writes in his influential book on antitrust that it has "long been clear . . . that antitrust deals with what are at root economic phenomena."[19] This can be understood both as a criticism of populist orientations to antitrust as well as a denial that antitrust invokes any significant moral issues (which he dismisses by arguing that economics' focus on efficiency is "an important social value" that "establishes a prima facie case for having an antitrust policy").[20] More precisely, legal scholar Herbert Hovenkamp, one of the premier current scholars of antitrust, declares in his own treatise on the topic that "antitrust is an economic, not a moral, enterprise."[21]

The problem with these statements is twofold. First, antitrust law is an exercise of power on behalf of the state, and therefore represents an intrinsically ethical, legal, and political matter, even if its implementation is based on economic theory. As Bork, a supporter of antitrust enforcement (albeit in a limited way) wrote, "Antitrust constitutes one of the most elaborate deployments of governmental force in areas of life still thought committed primarily to private choice and initiative."[22] As such, it necessarily invokes considerations of rights and justice, the primary focus of this book (and others).[23]

Second, and more important, economics itself is an intrinsically value-laden enterprise, both in its descriptive, scientific mode ("positive economics"), and even more obviously in its prescriptive, policy-oriented mode ("normative economics").[24] Economic models of individual decision-making assume certain ethical precepts on behalf of its agents, reflecting a particular ethical orientation, based on utilitarianism, that denies the important role of principles, duty, and commitment

7

in choice. Economists reveal the same utilitarian basis even more starkly when making policy recommendations, urging policies that maximize welfare with no consideration for underlying rights—such as the right to participate in commerce without being obligated to promote the general welfare. Even if antitrust were simply an economic matter, divorced from its status as law, it would still not be "purely" economic in the sense of being amoral, for such a separation is impossible. Although traditional, populist approaches to antitrust are understood to be explicitly ethical in nature, the modern economic orientation to antitrust is no less based on moral values—different ones, to be sure, but equally opposed to the focus on rights and justice emphasized in this book.[25]

I maintain that this presumption about the "value-free" economics behind antitrust, in combination with a misunderstanding about the nature of markets and commerce, accounts for the widespread acceptance of antitrust as a "merely" technocratic exercise of regulation.[26] After all, if business owners are seen as lesser participants in a market economy, mere means to the ultimate end of consumer well-being, and economists can use "scientific techniques" to tell the government how to make firms serve this end even better, with no relevant ethical considerations arguing against them, then antitrust would seem obviously good and right. As I shall explain throughout this book, these assumptions are incorrect, so the conclusions do not follow—and a focus on rights will show that they are wrong.

THE PLAN GOING FORWARD

Although the borders are fuzzy at best, in the rest of this book I follow a path that begins with economics, later working philosophy into discussion, and bringing in law near the end, explaining each new topic as it becomes necessary. (Some of the material I cover may be familiar, depending on your background, but there's a good chance my presentation of it will be different than what you're used to.)

I start in Chapter 2 by laying out the standard economics behind the modern conception of antitrust. I explain how the interaction between buyers and sellers in markets generate benefit for both parties, which adds up to total welfare. Next, I show how competition generates prices, how a higher level of competition generally leads to higher welfare, and how this motivates antitrust's focus on discouraging, preventing, or punishing anticompetitive behavior, especially collusive price-fixing, merger, and restraints of trade.

In Chapter 3 I challenge the ethical foundations of the economics of antitrust. Here I introduce utilitarianism, which underlies mainstream economic theory—especially welfare economics, which provides the justification for antitrust law and enforcement. Next I explain some problems with utilitarianism that should give us pause, including its neglect of rights, and as an alternative I introduce deontology, a school of ethics most often associated with Immanuel Kant, which provides a solid grounding for our focus on rights in the next chapter.

The spotlight turns more directly to philosophy in Chapter 4 when I introduce the conception of rights I use in the book—and property rights in particular—which I argue is a moderate and familiar one. After explaining why rights are so important, especially in a field of study and policy dominated by utilitarianism, I ask what rights the various parties to a market transaction—specifically, business owners and consumers—have, and how our understanding of antitrust might change if rights are taken seriously. This focus continues in Chapter 5 as we revisit the three main categories of antitrust violations—collusive price-fixing, merger, and exclusionary practices—in terms of rights rather than utility or welfare, which paints a rather different picture than is normally seen in discussions of antitrust and competition law.

We introduce concepts from law in Chapter 6 as we showcase the distinction between harm and wrong, which is not acknowledged in economics (or utilitarianism) but is recognized and emphasized in traditional understandings of the law. I start by exploring a simple concept from economics, externalities, that ignores this distinction, after which I show how the introduction of rights makes the problem with them clear—and how the law offers a simple solution. I shall show how this problem is pervasive throughout the economic approach to the law in general and the economics of antitrust in particular. Finally, this leads us into a discussion of the differences between tort (accident) law and criminal law, which is relevant to both externalities and antitrust, due to the neglect of meaningful rights in both.

In Chapter 7 we bring the economics, philosophy, and law together to explore deeper issues with the standard justifications for antitrust in light of the distinction between harm and wrong and the neglect of rights that obscures it—including a possible justification that both addresses harm and respects property rights. Finally, in Chapter 8, we pull back from the narrow focus to look at the essential nature of markets and competition in general, exploring how they look in the context of a meaningful treatment of rights and what this perspective means for government intervention in the economy.

Before we move on, I want to make two qualifications in anticipation of likely (and understandable) reactions to the overview above.

First, although I expect libertarians and classic liberals to be more likely than anyone to be receptive to my argument, I firmly believe it should appeal more broadly to people of various political stances, even those that favor a more active role for the government in the economy. Although liberals and conservatives emphasize different rights, they all take rights seriously—and here I argue merely that this should include the property rights of business owners, understood in a moderate sense that acknowledges limitations in the interest of competing rights. Government may want to increase the total well-being of their citizens, and there are many legitimate ways to do this, but they should not come at the expense of rights (which is exactly what rights exist for). Furthermore, although I give the benefit of the doubt to antitrust authorities that they are honestly pursuing consumer well-being or welfare in general, political figures often accuse the other side of abusing antitrust enforcement for illicit ends—and to the extent these accusations are sincere, a reduced scale and scope of antitrust power would help to ameliorate these concerns.

Second, I fully expect to be accused of shilling for "Big Business." Yes, I do argue that the property rights of business owners should be protected more than they currently are. But I also maintain that these rights should be used only when that use does not violate the equally valid rights of others. Although I argue that the actions that violate antitrust law do not violate anyone else's rights, actions that *do* violate rights—including fraud, deceit, and coercion, as well as more general areas of criminal activity—are wrong, both morally and legally, and should be dealt with accordingly. If anything, the enforcement resources currently absorbed by the antitrust divisions around the world would be freed up under my proposal to address *actual wrongs* perpetrated by those in the business community. In other words, I'm not trying to let anybody off the hook for wrongdoing—I'm trying to clear up what wrongdoing is and is not, so resources can be directed in more effective and ethical ways.

2

The economics of antitrust

As we saw in the last chapter, the most common interpretation of antitrust today is explicitly economic in nature, based on maximizing the benefit to consumers (or society as a whole). Although this was not the motivation of those who wrote the original antitrust laws (or the Neo-Brandeisian revivalists), who were more focused on limiting corporate size and concentration, the consensus today remains that antitrust should focus on economic concerns, specifically the effects on firm behavior on welfare or efficiency.

In this chapter I shall survey the economics behind antitrust, not only because it is the mainstream understanding, but also because many of the issues I identify in antitrust are embedded in the economic analysis itself. If economics is new to you, I hope you find my explanation intuitive and non-technical, free of the customary graphs and math. (If you are familiar with economics already, you may find my treatment interesting for the same reason.) My goal is to introduce the basic economic rationale for antitrust, focusing on only the elements necessary for the philosophical arguments I shall introduce in the next chapter.

WELFARE AND SURPLUS

The field of economics can be divided into two parts: *positive economics*, which describes the behavior of individuals, institutions, and the economy as a whole, and *normative economics*, which makes recommendations to improve the outcomes of this behavior based on some goal (whether implicit or explicit). Although antitrust has relied for the past half century on the positive economics of firm behavior and market outcomes (a field known as industrial organization), the legal and policy-oriented side of antitrust falls squarely within normative economics.[1]

Within normative economics, antitrust is an application of *welfare economics*, which aims to maximize the total welfare of the members of society.[2] In the context of commercial activity, economists define welfare as the sum of the well-being of all participants in the market, or the total benefit of commerce to buyers and sellers, net of the costs to both. This is easier to see on the producer side: their benefit is the revenue they earn from selling goods and services, and their costs include wages and salaries, rent, utilities, and the cost of raw materials. When we subtract costs from benefits, we get their net benefit, which we know better as *profit*.

Things are somewhat more abstract when we turn to the consumer side: their costs are the prices they pay for goods and services, which is clear, but the benefit they get from these things is inherently subjective. Economists usually think of this benefit in terms of a consumer's *reservation price*, the maximum amount of money they would be willing to pay for a particular good or services. For example, suppose I go to my local bookstore for the latest novel by my favorite author, for which I am willing to pay up to $30. Assuming I'm sincere about how much I value the book, this means it is worth $30 to me; I would be happy to pay less but I would not be willing to pay more. Therefore, $30 is my reservation price for the book, the largest amount of money I am willing to exchange for it, which is one way to represent the value I place on it—or the benefit I get from buying it.

Suppose I arrive at the bookstore (or its website) and discover the book costs only $20. We can assume I would buy it, because the bookstore is asking for less than my reservation price. What's more, after buying it, I will have made my own kind of "profit," or what economists call *consumer surplus*. In this case, my consumer surplus is $10 because, after paying $20 for a book I was willing to pay $30 for, I leave the store with $10 I would have been willing to give up for the book but didn't have to, which I can now spend on something else that provides me additional benefit. (This is the economic logic behind the common-sense idea that lower prices make consumers better off.)

Other consumers have different reservation prices, which changes their consumer surplus. Someone with the higher reservation price of $25 would still buy the book, but they would realize only $5 of consumer surplus; someone else with a reservation price of $20 would break even, receiving zero consumer surplus, assuming they buy the book at all. (Technically, they would be indifferent about buying the book, because they would be exchanging $20 for something worth exactly $20 to them.) But consumers with a reservation price of less than $20 would not buy the book at this price; instead, they might look elsewhere for a lower price, wait until the price falls to their reservation price, or buy a comparable but cheaper book. If they did buy the book for $20, they would have lost value, paying more than the book was worth to them, and incurring consumer loss rather than surplus.

If we sum up the amounts of surplus realized by all the consumers who buy a product, we get the total consumer surplus in that market, which parallels the total producer surplus (profit) earned by the firms supplying the product. Understood this way, we see that the concepts of surplus for consumer and producers are similar: both groups enjoy benefits and incur costs from the exchange of money for goods and services. Also, the two surpluses are connected because the price paid by consumers (their cost) is the same price received by producers (their benefit), a fact that will become important later.

Together, consumer surplus and profit combine to equal total surplus, also known as welfare, which is the concept that policy-oriented economists, including those who work on antitrust, try to maximize (at least in theory). Markets can achieve maximum welfare if every unit of output that generates any surplus is produced and sold, and no units are produced or sold that would generate losses (or negative surplus). Ideally, every unit of output that is produced and sold leads to a certain amount of surplus for the consumer who bought it and a certain amount of profit for the firm that produced it. As long as consumers are willing to buy more output and producers are willing to make more output—in other words, as long as both parties see more benefit than cost from the additional commerce—then additional output will increase total welfare.

There are, however, natural forces that set limits on this process, implying an upper bound to how much additional output will generate additional welfare. On the consumption side, the standard psychological assumption of *diminishing marginal utility* says that any person's desire for a given product is limited: due to satiation, boredom, or a simple taste for variety, consumers derive less value from extra units of a given product the more of it they consume. This is reflected in a decline in their reservation prices as they buy more of a product. For instance, you may be willing to pay $10 for a terrific burrito, but you may not be willing to pay $10 for a second one, at least not right away—but you might be willing to pay $5 for it. Diminishing marginal benefit works across different consumers as well. If we assume the consumer who value a product the most will be the first in line to buy it, we can rank consumers by how much they value a product. As more of a product is sold, each consumer's reservation price would be lower than the last, as if they were all one consumer buying varying amounts of the same product.

The opposite happens with costs on the production side, even if the financial cost of resources stays the same. As more production resources are devoted to increasing output of one product, the firm incurs greater sacrifice in terms of foregone output of other products (which are also profitable). Imagine a clothing manufacturer that retools its factory to produce more dresses at the expense of blouses, or an automotive manufacturer that adapts its assembly line to make more trucks and fewer cars: as these changes are made, presumably to take advantage of higher potential profit, they also involve an increasing level of sacrifice in terms of the foregone profit from the output reduced. In other words, companies face rising opportunity costs for their resources, implying that production costs rise as output increases, even if the cost of production measured in money remains the same.[3]

If we combine these two effects, we find that as more of a particular good or service is produced and sold, consumers' benefit from an extra unit (or *marginal benefit*) falls and producers' cost of making an extra unit (or *marginal cost*) rises, squeezing the surplus going to both parties. One copy of a book sold may have a marginal benefit to that consumer of $30 and a marginal cost to the producer of $10, resulting in $20 total surplus. The next book sold, whether to the same consumer or another one who values it a little less, may have a marginal benefit of $29 and a marginal cost of production of $11, resulting in only $18 of total surplus—smaller than $20 because of diminishing marginal benefit and increasing marginal cost.

We also see now that the price at which the product is exchanged, which we know is both the cost to consumers and the benefit to producers, is a wash in terms of total surplus because it is simply a transfer from one party to another. Consider the first copy of the book sold above: if it is sold for $20, the consumer and the producer each get $10 of surplus, but if it is sold for $25, the producer gets $15 in profit and the consumer get $5 in surplus. Nonetheless, the total surplus is the same $20 regardless of the price, which is all that matters as far as welfare maximization is concerned. In other words, the only thing that is relevant to total surplus is the difference between the consumers' marginal benefit and the producer's marginal cost.[4]

As long as there is still some surplus from additional output, producing and selling it will add to welfare, but diminishing marginal benefit and increasing marginal cost imply that we will eventually reach the limit we mentioned above. As more output is produced and sold, eventually marginal benefit and marginal cost will meet in the middle, at which point the total surplus from an additional unit of output vanishes. For example, as more books are produced and sold, we may reach a copy that costs $20 to produce and the next consumer's reservation price is $20. At this point, neither would gain any surplus from that book. (The price would have to be $20 as well, and neither party would find this price worthwhile to motivate their side of the exchange.) Even if that copy were made and sold, any further copies of the book would generate negative surplus because the cost of production would be higher than the extra benefit to consumers. Imagine the next copy of the book costs $21 to produce but is worth only $19 to the next consumer.

If it were made and sold (for some mysterious reason), that book would generate $19 of value at a cost of $21, reducing total welfare by $2—and things would only get worse from there, as marginal cost continues to rise and marginal benefit continues to fall.

Therefore, total welfare is maximized when the *optimal* level of output is made and sold, or where the last unit produced and sold is valued by consumers exactly as much as it cost producers. In economic terms, this is the point at which the *marginal benefit* to consumers equals the *marginal cost* to firms—or, recognizing that consumers and producers are all participants in the market and the economy, we can simply say this is where marginal benefit equals marginal cost. Any lesser amount of output would leave unrealized surplus on the table, and any greater amount would result in losses that would reduce total surplus. The optimal output is the top of the welfare hill, so to speak, and welfare falls if more or less output than the optimal level is traded.[5]

PRICES AND COMPETITION

It's one thing to show what it means for welfare to be maximized and what the optimal amount of output looks like, but another thing to say what leads the participants in the market to exchange that level of output. In a market economy, this is done by the price, which has to give incentive for both producers to make the optimal level output and for consumers to buy that output. If the price is too high, producers would happily make more, because their potential surplus would be higher on each unit, but consumers would not buy it, because their reservation price will more quickly fall to the higher price (at which point they stop buying). If the price is too low, the situation is reversed: consumers would like to buy more, because it takes longer for their reservation price to fall to the lower price, but producers will not be willing to produce as much because there is less profit margin per unit.

Between higher prices, which lead producers to make more than consumers want to buy, and lower prices, which lead producers to make less than consumers want to buy, we expect there to be a price that gets producers to make exactly as much as consumers want to buy. This would be the price at which the consumers' reservation price for the last unit equals the producers' extra cost of making it—in other words, where marginal benefit equals marginal cost, and the optimal, welfare-maximizing level of output is produced. Only at this price will consumer and producer behavior perfectly balance each other, "clearing" the market (which is why this is sometimes called the *market-clearing price*).

How do we get to this market-clearing price? Does the government bring this price about? Can they first determine what it is and then simply impose it on consumers and producers, thereby ensuring that welfare is maximized? After the socialist calculation debate of the early twentieth century, the consensus is no. Although it may be theoretically possible for central planners to calculate the price that leads to the optimal level of output *if* they possessed all the necessary information, there is no way for them to access and acquire this information, given that it's private, subjective, and dynamic. They would need to know the reservation costs of every consumer for every level of consumption of every good and service, along with detailed information about the production process of every company, including the opportunity costs involved in the choice between alternate products. Even in an age of nearly infinite data storage and computing power, the nature of the information required is such that it would be impossible to collect, much less process.[6]

Fortunately, top-down planning is not necessary, because the market-clearing price can be reached through the operation of the market itself. In his classic paper "The Use of Information in Society," economist Friedrich von Hayek explained how the market generates all the information necessary for its operation through buyers and sellers using their private knowledge to make their own individual decisions, without needing any one person or group in society to have all that information.[7] No one other than John needs to know how much he values a new sweater; only he needs to know, and then he makes his own consumption decisions based on that subjective knowledge. Likewise, no one other than Jane needs to know how much it costs her small company to produce a sweater; only she needs to know, and then she makes production decisions based on that cost. If consumers buy output whenever the price they have to pay is below their reservation prices, and firms supply products whenever the price they can charge is above their cost, then every unit of a product that is produced and purchased will add to total welfare—and the market-clearing price, and with it the optimal, welfare-maximizing level of output, can be reached without anyone having to calculate and impose it from on high.

Note that I said the optimal price *can* be reached; I have not yet explained when or how it happens. The only thing the process above guarantees is that any output made and bought will add to total welfare, because producers will only make output that adds to their profit and consumers will only buy output that leaves them consumer surplus. This does not guarantee, however, that the *optimal* amount of output will be produced; this depends on market conditions that together lead to what economists call *perfect competition*.

In the mathematical terms of economics, the state of perfect competition requires a number of unrealistic conditions that, nonetheless, are useful for understanding what the "ultimate" level of competition would look like. For instance, there must be an infinitely large number of infinitely small buyers and sellers, all of whom deal in an identical product. All buyers and sellers must know everything about the products produced by all of the sellers, as well as the prices each of them charges. Finally, it must be costless to enter or leave the market, which admittedly is more of an issue for producers than consumers.

Together, these conditions create an environment of intense competition in which each of the many tiny firms selling an identical product must accept whatever the going market price is, or lose whatever few sales they have to their competitors because buyers know all the prices charged and will avoid any firm charging even a slightly higher price. (Because all buyers also know that all firms' products are identical, no firm can justify a higher price based on its product being better or different.) Given the prevailing market price, new firms will enter the market as long as that price covers their cost, which includes their opportunity cost, or the profit they could expect in the next-best use of their resources (often called *normal profits*). As more firms enter the industry, the market price gradually falls to cost, at which point no new firms enter (because the opportunity to earn more than their alternative level of profit has disappeared).

In the end, just enough firms enter the market to produce output to satisfy all consumer demand at a price that is driven down to cost by competitive pressures, guaranteeing that *any* output that would increase welfare is produced. Such a market would never leave unrealized surplus on the table; if there is any consumer demand that can be met at a profit, no matter how small, a firm will enter the market or expand output to meet that demand, until no more consumers can be satisfied at a profit to any firm. Because all opportunities for increasing surplus are exhausted, a perfect competitive market maximizes welfare.

As I described it above, perfect competition is a mathematical ideal: each firm is essentially a geometric point with no mass or size, operating in a market with no frictions (such as entry costs) or market realities (such as even the slightest differences between products). This is the way economics professors teach the concept, albeit usually with graphs or math, because the logic is straightforward and the results are clear: perfect competition ensures that welfare is maximized, consumers enjoy all the output they want at the lowest price possible, and firms make no more than "normal profits," merely covering all their costs (including production costs and the profits they could have earned elsewhere).

Because it's a mathematical ideal, perfect competition can never obtain in the real world, but that does not deny the concept a useful role as a benchmark. As a real-world industry approaches any of the conditions of perfect competition, we would expect price to fall and welfare and output to increase. With respect to policy, then, the practical focus is on the degree and quality of competition in a market, wherein more competition, all else the same, is regarded as good for consumers and society in general, while leaving business owners a sustainable level of profit (matching if not exceeding what they could make in alternative pursuits).

MONOPOLY

Anything that restrains competition in a market, accordingly, has the opposite effects, with monopoly being at the other end of the spectrum from perfect competition. In mathematical terms, monopoly is just as extreme and unrealistic as perfect competition, but is defined much more simply: a single firm producing a unique product with *no* substitutes.

Many industries are characterized as monopolies, usually when there is one clearly dominant firm, but the absence of substitutes—which represent competition for a firm's product—is essential to declare a firm a monopoly in a meaningful sense. This is where things become complicated, because substitution is in the eye of the beholder, depending on consumer sentiment and use, with cost often playing a key factor. For example, traditionally—or at least as jewelers would like us to believe—there is no substitute for a diamond in an engagement ring, but couples have certainly made do with other stones in a pinch. Whether a firm's product has substitutes also depends on market definition: Coca-Cola has no substitutes in the market for Coca-Cola, several in the market for colas, even more in the market for soda (or "pop", if you prefer), and countless substitutes in the market for beverages in general. A complete absence of substitutes is extremely rare, rendering the technical definition of monopoly as unattainable as perfect competition. As with perfect competition, however, monopoly remains a useful concept as a benchmark representing the other extreme of the competition spectrum.

For practical purposes, we can understand monopoly as a single firm selling a product with *few close* substitutes, which captures the important point that the absence of substantial market competition grants the monopolistic firm some degree of discretion over price.[8] As we saw, each firm in a perfectly competitive industry faces so many others selling a product identical to theirs, and perfectly knowledgeable consumers to boot, that no one firm has the ability to raise their price even slightly above the going market price. With their lack of substantial competition, monopolists are free to increase their prices without

THE ECONOMICS OF ANTITRUST

fear of losing sales to competitors. They will, of course, lose some sales to existing customers with low reservation prices: although monopolists sell products with few substitutes, they are not necessarily essential products, and some consumers can simply choose not to buy them at all if the price is too high. Even so, the monopolist's profit can increase as long as the increase in revenue on the units sold at the higher price is larger than the fall in revenue from lost sales. For example, if the firm raises its price by 10 per cent and only loses 5 per cent of its sales, revenues will increase (and total costs will fall due to the lower output produced).

There is a limit to this process, however: eventually, the firm raises its price so high that the revenue lost from departed customers will exceed the extra revenue made off their remaining customers. If the firm from our example later raises its price by another 10 per cent, and this time loses 15 per cent of its sales, its revenue falls (which the decrease in costs will only partially offset). Eventually the monopolist realizes that, during its gradual process of increasing price little by little, a 10 per cent increase in price lowers its sales by 10 per cent, exactly negating the positive effect of the higher price, and so there it stops. At that point, the monopolist has reached the price that maximizes its profit—or its own "optimum," if you will. This price will be higher than the price under perfect competition, possibly significantly higher, but not "as high as they can," at least not how that is often understood and meant. Monopolists have the ability to raise the price as high as they want, certainly, but there is an upper bound to how high they will want it to be. Even in the lack of competition, the monopolist is still subject to consumer demand, and this ensures that they will not raise price so high that they will lose money.

How do the outcomes of a market under perfect competition and monopoly compare, all else the same? Due to the absence of competitive pressures, a monopolist will earn a higher level of profit than all the firms in perfect competition put together. Furthermore, because of the lower level of output and the higher price they pay for it, consumers enjoy less surplus. If profit is higher and consumer surplus is lower, what happens to total welfare?

We don't need to calculate and compare the contrasting effects on welfare, because we know that a monopoly produces a suboptimal level of output, which implies that potential surplus or welfare is left on the table. True, the higher price means that some surplus from the output that is produced is shifted from consumers to the monopolist. This is a distributional aspect of monopoly that can be used to support a stronger focus on consumer surplus in antitrust enforcement, but as a mere transfer it has no effect on total welfare; the losses to consumers become gains for the monopolist. Rather, it is the loss in total surplus due to suboptimal output that represents the general welfare loss from monopoly. Consumers value additional units of output more than it would cost the firm to produce them; in other words, at the point the monopolist stops producing, marginal benefit is higher than marginal cost. But the monopolist will never produce any output above its own "optimal" profit-maximizing level because they lose more revenue from lowering the price than they earn from additional sales. The welfare that goes unrealized under monopoly compared to perfect competition is called *deadweight loss*: surplus that is there for the taking if only output were increased. This would require competitive pressures that do not exist in a state of monopoly (but which antitrust naturally seeks to restore).

As we have seen, perfect competition and monopoly, when defined mathematically, are unrealistic extremes at either end of a range of competitiveness, with any real-world industry falling somewhere in the middle. Starting from the monopolistic end of the range, competition increases either when new firms enter the market for the product the monopolist produces, or consumers embrace new substitutes for it (produced by other firms). Whatever the cause, the monopolist sees less demand for its product and loses some of its ability to raise its price without losing sales to its new competitors. As a result of the increased competition, prices fall and output rises, lowering profit and increasing consumer surplus, which together increase total welfare as the dead-weight loss from suboptimal output shrinks.

The process works the other way from the perfectly competitive end of the spectrum. The possible causes are many, all of which involve a compromise in one or more of the conditions for perfect competition. Some of the tiny firms may consolidate, resulting in fewer, larger firms with more influence over price. Firms may differentiate their products, making them less substitutable from consumers' point of view, which grants their producers more leeway to raise prices for their newly "unique" products. Costs of entering the market may rise, insulating the existing firms to some degree from competitive pressure. Information may become more difficult to get, so consumers cannot as easily discover when one firm is charging higher prices than others. In any of these cases, firms begin to realize some discretion over prices after capturing a tiny bit of the market for themselves; after they begin to raise prices, total output falls, increasing profits while decreasing consumer surplus, lowering total welfare (and creating deadweight loss that grows as the process continues).

The latter process is what antitrust authorities want to prevent, especially if the market is considered substantially uncompetitive to begin with and welfare is already well below the perfectly competitive maximum. A very competitive market that threatens to become slightly less competitive is of less concern than an uncompetitive market becoming more so. (The effects on welfare from a merger of two firms among twenty is negligible, but a merger of two firms among three is a different matter.) Generally, insofar as authorities want to ensure that welfare or consumer surplus is maximized, they would want to encourage firm behavior that brings an industry closer to the ideal of perfect competition and discourage firm behavior that brings it closer to monopoly.[9]

This explains why many economically-oriented antitrust scholars are ambivalent about whether they should focus on maximizing total welfare in general or consumer surplus in particular. In the simple analysis presented above, when an industry becomes more competitive, output increases, which increases total welfare. At the same time, more of that growing total surplus is transferred from producers, whose profits fall due to more competition, to consumers, who enjoy more output at lower prices. As long as increases in total welfare and consumer surplus (both resulting from higher output) go hand in hand, there seems to be little practical reason to distinguish between them when discussing policy or law. However, matters become more complicated if, for example, a merger that lessens competition also generates cost efficiencies, which may lead to greater profits even as output falls (with uncertain effect on prices). In such a case, it is possible that total welfare could rise while consumer surplus falls, and the response from anti-trust scholars and authorities would reveal whether their focus is on the entire economy or the consumers within it.[10]

ANTITRUST

The economic theory of competition laid out above provides the rationale for mainstream antitrust scholars and officials to restrict anticompetitive behavior: to prevent a slide towards monopolization that would lower consumer surplus and total welfare. Antitrust scholar Jonathan Baker puts it succinctly in his article "The Case for Antitrust Enforcement" when he identifies "the central role of antitrust" as "pro-tecting consumers against anticompetitive conduct that raises prices, reduces output, and hinders innovation and economic growth."[11]

In these terms, the economic logic of the most common targets of antitrust law is clear. For example, mergers between firms compet-ing in the same market and selling to the same consumers—known as *horizontal mergers*—are questioned because, as described above, having fewer firms in an industry would be expected to lead to lower output, higher prices, and less consumer surplus and total welfare (unless the mergers generate sufficient cost savings among the new post-merger firm to offset these effects). On the other hand, mergers between firms at different levels of the production process—known as *vertical mergers*—are less often questioned because they are regarded as having little impact on competition at either level. Instead, they are usually motiv-ated by cost savings in both markets that may lead to lower prices, more output, and higher consumer surplus and total welfare. Although economically-oriented antitrust scholars focus on horizontal mergers because of their more obvious and direct anticompetitive effects, the Neo-Brandeisians, who focus on broader societal and political goals

26

of antitrust, emphasize the dangers of vertical mergers as well because they contribute to increasing corporate size, power, and influence.[12]

Antitrust authorities also target other firm behaviors that have a more direct impact on market outcomes. The most obvious one is collusion between firms to fix prices above the competitive level in the industry, with clear and predictable effects on output, consumer surplus, and welfare. The same effect results from other examples of interference with the flexible adjustment of prices, such as *resale price maintenance*, wherein producers mandate a minimum price at which retailers may sell their product.[13]

Other pricing behaviors are more strategic, such as *predatory pricing*, in which a larger, more cost-efficient firm in a market lowers its price below a smaller, less efficient firm's cost to drive the latter out of business, after which the larger firm takes advantage of the lesser competition it engineered by raising its price once again. There is significant debate whether this is feasible as a long-run strategy, and therefore how much of a threat it poses to competition. The evidentiary burdens on antitrust enforcers are also higher in such cases, considering that for significant periods of time, lower prices will be maintained, increasing consumer surplus and total welfare, forcing the authorities to argue that the apparently pro-consumer behavior at the current time is actually anti-consumer in the long run.[14] Even monopolists may have reason not to keep their prices at the profit-maximizing level if they fear it will attract competitors or drive consumers to seek out substitute products; in such cases, "potential competition" may be sufficient to temper monopoly pricing to some degree.[15]

Abstracting from price itself, the general category of *exclusionary practices* in antitrust law, which refers to any actions by a firm to limit the output of other firms, reflects the concerns of antitrust scholars and officials who focus on economic outcomes. Because both consumer surplus and total welfare are maximized at a certain level of output, any behavior that reduces that output reduces both measures of well-being. Put another way, because perfect competition (ideally) generates the welfare-maximizing level of output and price, any restraint of trade is by implication anticompetitive in that it compromises this goal. Even recognizing that every real-world industry is, to some degree, necessarily uncompetitive compared to the ideal benchmark of perfect competition, behaviors that move the market in the direction of less competition, lower output, and higher prices is going to trigger antitrust attention.

I have no need to challenge the economic analysis of antitrust as I have presented it here. All of what I've written in this chapter is the standard economic treatment and defense of antitrust enforcement, which makes sense given the rationale of welfare maximization and the government's role therein—both of which I *do* challenge in the coming pages).

Furthermore, reality bears out the economic theory. As Baker notes after surveying the effects of antitrust enforcement:

> This evidence plainly suggests that in the absence of antitrust rules, anticompetitive conduct would often take place.... This evidence, too, suggests that absent antitrust enforcement, many industries would find ways of coordinating to the detriment of consumers and economic welfare.... In sum, studies of firm behavior ... demonstrate that without antitrust, firms can and do exercise market power, to the detriment of consumers and other buyers.[16]

I readily concede that the behaviors regulated or forbidden by antitrust authorities have very predictable and significantly deleterious effects on the well-being of consumers, as well as the efficiency of the economy as a whole. (The scale of these effects, however, is less certain, as we discuss in Chapter 7.)

What I *am* questioning, beginning in the next chapter, is the ethical relevance of these standards themselves. I am challenging the positions that welfare economics captures what is morally important to policy decisions and that the government has the right based on welfare economics to interfere in firm behavior, both of which the mainstream economic view of the market accepts uncritically and unreflectively.

In criticizing the basis of antitrust, I shall also show that the ethical presuppositions of mainstream economics lead to morally counter-intuitive results—and the fact that one of these results is a widely accepted area of regulatory law only shows how prevalent this economic view has become.

3

The ethics of economics

The central problem that I identify in antitrust is that it punishes actions that, although they may create harm, do not involve any wrong-doing. For instance, Raju Parakkal and Sherry Bartz-Marvez write that antitrust law "is primarily intended to restrain large firms from engaging in anticompetitive behavior that is not only detrimental to other firms but for the most part deleterious to the interests of con-sumers across the economy."[1] Like similar statements quoted earlier, this addresses the negative consequences of anticompetitive behavior, but makes no reference to any moral wrongdoing. The underlying idea is that all harm is equally problematic and needs to be minimized (or optimized with respect to benefit), regardless of any consideration of whether the actions that brought them about are wrongful in the sense of violating rights.

This is an intrinsic, pervasive, but largely unacknowledged problem with mainstream economics in general—and ultimately a legacy of its roots in the moral philosophy known as *utilitarianism*, with which we begin this chapter examining the ethical foundations of economics.[2] After introducing the basic tenets of utilitarianism and explaining how they relate to economics, I'll discuss the implications of their neglect of meaningful rights, turning to another school of ethics to fill that gap before we discuss rights in more detail in the next chapter.

UTILITARIANISM

The basic concept of utilitarianism can be traced back to antiquity, but its most well-known and modern presentation is due to the philosopher Jeremy Bentham, with important elaboration done by philosopher and economist John Stuart Mill.[3] Both men were reformers who recommended utilitarianism as a tool for social betterment through government policy and law, as well as a way of individuals to live an ethical life. In its most basic form, utilitarianism focuses on maximizing the total happiness, well-being, or *utility* of the members of a group or society. As such, it is a specific form of *consequentialism*, the general term for any ethical system that places moral value on the results or outcomes of actions, rather than those that focus on the moral status of actions themselves (such as *deontology*) or the character of the persons performing them (such as *virtue ethics*).[4]

According to the modern-day economist and philosopher Amartya Sen, utilitarianism has two essential aspects: it defines total utility as the sum of individuals' utilities, which it then puts forth as the particular consequence to be valued and maximized.[5] The definition of total utility reflects utilitarians' principled stance on moral equality, in which each and every person's utility counts equally in the sum, regardless of race, religion, gender, or class. This was an admirable and courageous statement to make in the days when Bentham and Mill wrote (and, unfortunately, all too often in our own). As we shall soon see, however, utilitarians' recognition of moral equality has a negative side as well: because it regards each person's utility as equally valid in the sum, it also regards each person's utility as substitutable for that of any other, and therefore potentially disposable.

At the very beginning of his treatise on utilitarianism, Bentham famously wrote: "Nature has placed mankind under the governance of two sovereign masters, *pain* and *pleasure*. It is for them alone to point out what we ought to do, as well as to determine what we shall do."[6] Bentham meant this to apply to decisions made by both individuals in their private lives as well as government actors in their official ones, asking everyone to think of the effects of their decisions on the well-being of others (as well as themselves).

Bentham's "pleasure" and "pain" easily translate into benefit and cost in the formal modeling of mainstream economics, in both its descriptive (positive) and prescriptive (normative) forms.[7] In descriptive terms, when economists try to understand and predict behavior, decision-makers are presumed to make choices that maximize their welfare or utility as represented by their preferences. This is most apparent in how economics considers the choices made by individuals: consumers spend money in order to satisfy their preferences for goods and services, workers devote time to labor in such a way to satisfy their preferences for income and leisure, and so forth. Although individuals' own pain and pleasure is assumed to dictate their choices, the part of Bentham's thought that urged the consideration of *other* people's well-being is usually left out of standard models, which instead assume self-interest on the part of individuals.[8]

Even institutions such as companies and government agencies are assumed to have preferences in a metaphorical sense: firms have a "preference" for profit, and government agencies have "preferences" for whatever their institutional purpose is (or, like bureaucracies in general, they have preferences for influence, size, and budget). In general, mainstream economics assumes that all agents make choices to further their preferences as much as possible within their constraints; in other words, they maximize their benefits net of cost, or maximize their personal welfare (which in this sense is merely a measure of preference-satisfaction). Stepping away from the formal language, this is just a fancier way of saying what Bentham wrote about pleasure versus pain determining "what we shall do" (even if it neglects his point about taking other people's pleasure and pain into account as well).

It is in the prescriptive realm of policymaking that mainstream economics more directly reflects the general spirit of Bentham's utilitarianism when it recommends that policymakers act to maximize total utility or welfare. We saw this in the last chapter when reviewing the welfare economics of markets and antitrust: the benefits of consumers and the profits of businesses are the "pleasure," their respective costs are the "pain," and the difference between them is total surplus or welfare, which comprises "what we ought to do" if we are the authorities in charge of regulating commerce (or any other matter of concern to the government). If other parties are affected by the trade between firms and consumers, as in the case of pollution resulting from the production or sale of the goods traded, their welfare must be considered as well. Such third-party effects are known as *externalities*, because the affected parties are outside of the transaction between producers and consumers; we shall discuss this in Chapter 6 (because they are not as straightforward as they seem, in terms of both economics and ethics).

Economics pursues the utilitarian goal of welfare maximization in several ways. A particularly abstract method that is useful when considering choices that affect society as a whole is to maximize a *social welfare function*. This is a technical construct that consolidates the preferences of all members of a society, resulting in a formula for total welfare, which authorities can then maximize by designing optimal policies, regulations, or laws.[9] Social welfare functions are useful for theoretical purposes, but in practice policymakers make such decisions with rough proxies for total welfare, such as gross domestic product and income per capita, each with their own attendant problems.[10]

When working on a smaller, incremental scale, where policy effects are limited to a narrow part of society such as a particular community or industry, economists can more easily measure and compare the amounts of "pleasure" and "pain" generated and engage in straightforward cost–benefit analysis. A specific form of cost–benefit analysis widely used in economics is known as *Kaldor–Hicks efficiency*, in which proposed policies are assessed to determine whether the total gains from the change exceed the total losses, even if the gains and losses accrue to different parties. We shall have more to say about Kaldor–Hicks efficiency below, because it is emblematic of many of the ethical issues with the utilitarian nature of economic policymaking.

The degree to which mainstream economics reflects and embodies its roots in classical utilitarianism stands in stark contradiction with the common belief that economics is value-free or "scientific," and therefore wholly separate from ethics—a popular misconception that, as we saw earlier, extends to antitrust economics as well. Some economists believe that utilitarianism is so obvious and "natural" that its presence in the foundations of economic theory hardly counts as ethics at all—after all, who could possibly argue against making everyone better off?[11] Of course, acknowledging the utilitarian legacy of economics does not imply that one has to disagree with it. Utilitarianism is a profoundly rich and intuitive approach to moral philosophy with a deep pedigree and many modern adherents who endorse its general approach to ethics while exploring its more nuanced aspects. Nonetheless, it does have its critics as well, and the problems they identify with utilitarians necessarily extend to economics as well.[12]

THE INDIVIDUAL IN UTILITARIANISM

The particular problem we are most concerned with is the failure of utilitarianism to acknowledge or respect what philosopher John Rawls called the "distinction between persons," which is lost when individuals are treated merely as contributors to total utility rather than as valuable in themselves.[13] As I indicated above, we can see this in the summing-up aspect of utilitarianism: although each person's utility is weighted equally in the total, it is also interchangeable with any other person's utility. If one person's utility can be sacrificed in such a way as to make others' utility rise by more, thereby increasing total utility or welfare, utilitarianism would endorse this procedure (as would the economic decision-making tool of Kaldor–Hicks efficiency). In the end, it does not matter that one person was helped only at the expense of another; all that matters is that the total amount of utility increased, not how the individual utilities that make up the total are distributed. In economics, the best evidence of this can be found in the mainstream's longtime failure to take issues of distributional justice and inequality seriously, choosing to focus more on the size of the economic pie than how its slices are apportioned among the population (which is one of the commonly cited problems with using GDP to represent national well-being).[14]

We also saw this in the previous chapter when we discussed the process by which an industry becomes less competitive. The deadweight loss resulting from a suboptimal level of output is taken more seriously than the shifting of the remaining surplus from consumers to producers due to the higher price. As an industry becomes more competitive, we see the reverse, with deadweight loss shrinking and total welfare growing as output rises and price falls. More precisely, welfare increases as total profit falls and consumer surplus rises by more, until the perfectly competitive ideal is reached, at which point consumer surplus is maximized and total profit merely covers opportunity costs. The result is an increase in total welfare and consumer surplus, which is celebrated, but at the expense of business owners, which is rarely even contemplated—and even if it were, their loss would be justified in a utilitarian fashion by the greater gain appreciated by consumers.

In general, this illustrates the problem with utilitarianism (and Kaldor–Hicks efficiency): as long as total welfare increases, it does not matter whether or how much anybody is harmed in the process. Put in the terms we used earlier, utilitarianism gives equal treatment to each person's utility, but this does not guarantee that the degree of treatment given to everyone is adequate or meaningful. Even though each person's utility is considered just as much as any other person's, no one's utility is taken especially seriously, and will quickly be sacrificed if other people's utility can be increased by more. In other words, to a utilitarian the greater good is always more important than the good of any one person, which is a noble sentiment when expressed by someone voluntarily making a sacrifice, but less so when that sacrifice is demanded from someone against their will (or in violation of their rights).[15]

Let's look at Kaldor–Hicks efficiency in more detail, starting with a simple example. Suppose a municipal planning committee is considering a proposal to build a new bridge over a river, which would benefit some people by a total of $10 million (through improved access, increased commerce, and shorter travel times) and harm others by a total of $8 million (through displacement of residents and commerce, as well as increased noise). Given these estimates, the bridge project would be considered efficient by the Kaldor–Hicks standard because the total benefits exceed the total costs, and therefore the "winners" gain enough to be able to compensate the "losers" and still be better off (by $2 million).

For this reason, Kaldor–Hicks efficient proposals are often called "potential Pareto improvements," invoking the more demanding criteria of *Pareto improvement*, which would reject any proposed change that makes *anyone* worse off in the process of benefiting others (in order to avoid making any sort of welfare comparisons between different persons). The term "potential" is key, however: the fact that the compensation in the Kaldor–Hicks case is purely theoretical, and rarely included in a proposal itself, implies that the "losers" most likely will be hurt and will not be compensated for the harm. In the words of legal philosopher Jules Coleman, the fact that Kaldor–Hicks efficient changes "are potentially Pareto superior has as much bearing on how they should be treated as the fact that I am potentially President of the United States has on how I should be treated now."[16] Because Pareto improvement is regarded as virtually unquestionable in economics and ethics, based on its implied respect for individual rights and well-being, framing Kaldor–Hicks efficient proposals as potential Pareto improvements comes off as a futile grasp for undeserved glory.[17]

There are several more problems with Kaldor–Hicks efficiency as it is normally implemented. One is its reliance on "willingness-to-pay" estimates, people's claims of what they would be willing to pay to have the policy approved (if they support it) or rejected (if they don't). Although these pledges are hypothetical, which is meant to allow those with limited resources to express their true valuations, they may still be biased if people are hesitant to "commit" more resources than they actually have. As a result, those with more wealth will be able and likely to claim higher amounts of benefit or harm than someone with less wealth, even if these claims are disproportionate to their actual predicted impacts—while they would also have disproportionate influence on the Kaldor–Hicks calculation. (For example, if those hurt by our bridge project were wealthier, their willingness-to-pay statements might overstate their personal impact from the bridge, which could sway the final decision in their favor, even if the actual impact on poorer communities is greater.) Once again, Jules Coleman summarized it well when he wrote that Kaldor–Hicks efficiency is "normatively prejudiced in a particularly insidious way: Namely, it turns out that what is efficient depends on what people are willing to pay, [which] in turn depends on what they are capable of paying. In short, the greater one's wealth, the more likely one is to increase it."[18]

However, it is a different issue with Kaldor–Hicks efficiency (and utilitarianism in general) that is more relevant to the argument of this book: the lack of concern for any rights belonging to the persons negatively affected by a policy change. The harms from a policy proposal are considered by Kaldor–Hicks efficiency to be merely a numerical counterweight to the benefits from it, and if the harms are smaller than benefits, the policy is declared efficient, with no further thought given to the parties on whom the harm is imposed.

Of course, compensation *could* be arranged. For instance, if land for the bridge construction is taken by the government under the doctrine of eminent domain, the landowners would be paid the going market rate for their property. However, not only may the payment be insufficient to compensate the landowner for the subjective value they place on the property, but more important, they would be denied the opportunity to refuse consent to the sale in the first place. "When we impose a Kaldor–Hicks improvement," wrote legal philosopher Jeremy Waldron, "we are not in any way honoring the voluntary consent of the losing party."[19] In other words, even if compensation were included in a Kaldor–Hicks proposal, and it was sufficient to make up for the full value of harms, the affected parties would still have been denied the right to refuse. As another legal philosopher, Ronald Dworkin, wrote, "the fact of self-interest in no way constitutes an actual consent."[20] (We shall hear more from Dworkin very soon.)

DEONTOLOGY AND RIGHTS

To put it bluntly, utilitarianism makes no room for rights, which Bentham famously called "nonsense upon stilts."[21] Utilitarians support rights only when they are justified by utilitarian concerns, which explains why many economists support property rights only insofar as they support the functioning of the market and the maximization of economic welfare. As Ronald Dworkin wrote critically of this position, "the institution of rights, and particular allocations of rights, are justified only insofar as they promote social wealth more effectively than other institutions or allocations."[22] Law scholar and economist Richard Posner argues that economics recognizes rights as important, but qualifies this when he writes that "the economist recommends the creation of such rights . . . when the cost of voluntary transactions is low," but "when transaction costs are prohibitive, the recognition of absolute rights is inefficient."[23] Posner exemplifies the utilitarian way of thinking about rights in making them contingent on being "efficient" and benefiting total welfare, rather than deriving from a moral principle or duty.

The problem with basing the justification of rights solely on utilitarian grounds is that it defeats the very purpose of rights: to protect the holder of the right from the demands of utilitarian reasoning. As Dworkin wrote in the introduction to his book *Taking Rights Seriously*: "Individual rights are political trumps held by individuals. Individuals have rights when, for some reason, a collective goal is not a sufficient justification for denying them what they wish, as individuals, to have or to do, or not a sufficient justification for imposing some loss or injury upon them."[24]

In this sense, rights absolve the persons who possess them from being forced to comply, at least in some instances, with the dictates of utilitarian policy. For the most part, citizens in liberal democracies are free to consume the goods and services they like, pursue the careers they find most personally fulfilling or lucrative, live where they want, and spend time with whomever they want, without having to think about the implications of their choices for total welfare or utility. By the same token, many of the rights granted to the people in the Bill of Rights to the U.S. Constitution protect certain ranges of behavior, such as speech, association, and religious practice, from suppression in the interests of overall well-being (which may be significantly affected, such as when a racist demagogue at a street corner offends decent passersby). Just as the First Amendment guarantee of freedom of speech is most valuable when it protects unpopular speech, the power of rights in general is most valuable when protecting individuals from being forced to benefit the greater good (whatever those in power believe that to be).

We shall discuss the positive aspects of rights at more length in Chapter 4, particularly in relation to firms' rights to conduct business in ways that do not necessarily maximize efficiency or welfare. For now, I shall focus on the consequences of their neglect in utilitarianism and economics in general, which reinforces the inherently ethical nature of economics while it highlights the limitations of that nature being limited to utilitarianism. To do this, it will be helpful to consider an ethical system often contrasted with utilitarianism: *deontology*.

Although there are many variations on the theme, deontology in general judges the morality of actions according to qualities intrinsic to the action itself, rather than by their consequences when performed in specific cases.[25] Accordingly, deontologists speak of actions with the absolute terms *right* or *wrong* instead of the utilitarian's relative terms of *good* and *bad*, because an action is declared moral and immoral in principle rather than having better or worse effects in particular circumstances.

For example, most utilitarians would say that lying in general is unethical, because the practice usually leads to negative outcomes overall, but they make room for "benevolent lies," such as white lies or lies of compassion, when they might do more good than bad. Most deontologists, on the other hand, would say lying is wrong on its face, regardless of the effects or intent of a particular act of lying, because it violates a basic moral principle (such as the value of truth or respect for others). Deontologists are open to exceptions in specific cases, but they would be based on recognizing a competing moral principle. For example, deontologists would normally say doctors should tell the truth to their patients and their loved ones, but when the truth would cause tremendous pain, a principle of compassion may overwhelm a principle supporting honesty. (Imagine a doctor being asked by grieving widows if their partners were in pain when they died—even if they were, the doctor might lie to spare the survivors undue pain themselves.) Utilitarians and deontologists can agree on the ethics of lying, and even on specific exceptions, but they do so for different reasons.[26]

The most famous deontologist, Immanuel Kant, based his ethical system on the concepts of *autonomy*, which is the capacity of persons to act morally even when their own interests and the influence of others tempt them to do otherwise, and *dignity*, the incalculable and incomparable value possessed by every autonomous person. From these ideas, Kant developed the *categorical imperative*, his formulation of "the moral law," which serves as a test for possible actions (or *maxims*), resulting in duties to abstain from those actions if they fail the "test." There are several versions of the categorical imperative, each giving a different perspective on morality but all technically equivalent (or so Kant claimed).[27]

It should be no surprise that lying fails the categorical imperative test in all its versions. The best-known version of the categorical imperative is "act only according to that maxim whereby you can at the same time will that it should become a universal law," which is basically a more formalized version of the question you likely heard as a child: "What if everyone did that?"[28] Lying fails this test because if everyone lied whenever it stood to benefit them, no one would believe anything anyone said, which would defeat the purpose of lying in the first place. In other words, lying is inconsistent with its own purpose when universalized, which results in a duty not to lie.

Although the universalization test seems more like an exercise in logic than ethics, keep in mind why we universalize our proposed actions in the first place: because it acknowledges the equivalent moral status of all persons, which denies us the right to use others as tools for our purposes. Based on this, we could also say that Kant held lying to be wrong because it uses the person lied to merely as a means to the liar's end, and thereby fails to respect their dignity as an end in themselves. This language comes from another version of the categorical imperative, which is more clearly ethical in nature: "Act in such a way that you treat humanity, whether in your own person or in the person of another, always at the same time as an end and never simply as a means."[29] In practice, this means we must not engage in acts such as deception or coercion, both of which deny the other person any meaningful consent in a situation that affects them, reducing them to a mere pawn in someone else's game. We might also think of this in terms of a right not to be treated this way, which is a *correlative right*, implied by (or correlated with) the duty not to do so.

It is in this context that the shortcomings of Kaldor–Hicks efficiency become more clear. When a policy is approved that benefits one group of people at the cost of harming another, the persons harmed are literally used as means to the ends of the persons benefited. (In the case of welfare maximization, *all* persons who are affected, whether they are helped or harmed, are used merely as means to that end, because total welfare is abstracted from any of them.) As described earlier, this violation of dignity stands even if compensation is given, because the persons harmed (and compensated) were not given the opportunity to deny consent. For this reason, as legal philosopher Anthony Kronman wrote, "for a Kantian, the Kaldor–Hicks test has no significance."[30] Even the Pareto improvement test, which requires that no one be harmed by a policy change, runs afoul of this Kantian principle when judgments of whether someone is "better off" or "worse off" are made by outside parties with no information regarding people's private valuations. This provides yet another reason to object to Kaldor–Hicks harms even when compensation is provided (as in the case of eminent domain takings).[31]

When those affected by policy decisions are not treated as persons with dignity, we see the dark side of utilitarianism in economic theory and policy: the well-being of some is sacrificed to increase the well-being of others (or the greater good as a whole), without regard for any duties prohibiting this or the rights implied by these duties. To be sure, this may not necessarily be inappropriate, such as when there are no rights to be violated. Consider two employees in a firm, who are competing for one promotion, with their manager deciding which employee will do more good for the firm if promoted. Because neither employee has a right to be promoted, whichever one is passed over for the other has not been wronged or denied respect (assuming they received due consideration). By the same token, a government agency awarding a contract to one of two firms does not wrong one by choosing the other, assuming again that they were both treated fairly in the process. It is only when the parties affected by a policy or law have acknowledged rights that are dismissed in the process of utilitarian calculation (such as cost–benefit analysis or Kaldor–Hicks efficiency) that an issue with the neglect of rights arises.

In the next chapter, I shall argue that antitrust law is a prime example of this neglect of valid recognized rights in a utilitarian or economic setting. Firms have property rights, both in their products as well as their own assets, which are disregarded in the government's attempt to engineer an increase in welfare and consumer surplus. Jonathan Baker explicitly uses cost–benefit analysis to defend antitrust enforcement, and concludes that "the benefits of antitrust enforcement to consumers and social welfare—particularly in deterring the harms from anticompetitive conduct across the economy—seem likely to be far larger than what the government spends on antitrust enforcement and firms spend directly or indirectly on antitrust compliance."[32] Although antitrust makes sense from this utilitarian perspective, it comes at the expense of the rights of business owners to use their property to engage in commerce, provided they break no laws concerning fraud, deceit, or coercion.

To my knowledge, defenders of antitrust have not explained why these rights deserve to be set aside in the interest of welfare and consumer surplus (although I shall consider some possible defenses later in the book). It could be justified, of course, if there were equally important rights on the part of consumers and competitors that legitimately blocked the exercise of business owners' property rights—but as we'll see in the next chapter, it is very difficult to identify or justify the existence of such rights. In their absence, the business activities prohibited by antitrust law may cause harm but violate no rights in the process, leading us to question (in Chapter 7) the role of antitrust enforcement in criminalizing action that is not wrongful.

4

Introducing rights

In liberal societies, everyone claims certain rights. Depending on where you live, you may have the right to free speech, the right of free worship, and the right to love and marry who you choose—all subject to limitations in acknowledgment of the rights of others (which, in extreme cases, are litigated in court or debated in legislatures). Different political parties and activist groups argue for the importance of certain rights over others, or that their constituents or members deserve more rights than other people do or more protection for their preferred rights when they conflict with others. Some argue that in the United States, more than any other democracy, rights are emphasized too much; as legal scholar Jamal Greene puts it, "rights are the commandments of our civil religion," and they are often presumed to stop a discussion rather than providing grounds for exploring it more deeply.[1]

A confusion over the nature and importance of rights also lies at the heart of the problems with antitrust, in which the traditionally protected rights of some parties are neglected at the same time that new, arbitrarily granted rights are implied to belong to other parties. In this chapter, we'll outline a basic conception of rights in general and property rights in particular, focusing on their importance as well as their limitations. Then we'll apply this conception to antitrust, beginning with exploring the specific rights firms and consumers have in the marketplace and what considerations legitimately limit the exercise of these rights. This will support the overall argument of this book that antitrust law penalizes firms, not for violating any rights held by consumers or competitors, but simply for failing to contribute to total welfare—exactly the requirement against which their property rights are meant to protect.

THE ESSENCE OF RIGHTS

The understanding of rights that I use in this book is very simple and moderate, and I expect that it is one that most readers will find reasonable and familiar. I am not using any precise or specific definition, but merely the concept of rights that Dworkin referred to when he described them as "trumps," writing (as we saw in Chapter 3) that "individuals have rights when, for some reason, a collective goal is not a sufficient justification for denying them what they wish, as individuals, to have or to do."[2] In other words, rights protect individuals from the demands of utilitarian policy, carving out a "sphere of autonomy" in which people are free to do as they choose, regardless of the effects of their actions on total welfare, provided they respect the same rights of others.

This conception of rights is very broad and general. As such, it does not specify which rights belong to which individuals in which circumstances. In more liberal societies people generally have more and stronger rights, or wider spheres of autonomy, although the precise delineation of these rights differs. It also does not specify how strong such rights must be, and it certainly does not claim that any rights are absolute; any particular right can be limited or overridden by another right, principle, or interest that is judged to be more important in a particular situation. Indeed, much of the work of court systems, especially at the appellate level, is to adjudicate between different rights claims and decide which is more important in specific circumstances.[3]

Nonetheless, in order to have any meaning whatsoever, a right must take precedence over the demands of welfare in some non-trivial cases. At the very least, a right should not be set aside any time its enforcement would lower welfare by any amount, no matter how small. This would defeat the purpose of the right itself, and should only happen when the injury to welfare is very large indeed (perhaps catastrophic). In most cases, rights should be limited only in observance of other rights, as embodied in the aphorism that opens the Preface to this book, "your rights end where mine begin" (which also implies a certain sphere of autonomy).

Although the language may be unfamiliar, I believe this is a very common and widely held view of rights: not absolute, but with significant power to stand up to utilitarian concerns, and usually limited only by other rights with equal validity and importance (and in rare cases by consequences when very large). This is how most civil rights are considered, including rights to free speech, association, and worship, as well as protections given to members of specific minority groups. These rights are protected and enforced even when doing so results in harm to others.

For example, speech can cause true harm, ranging from "mere" offense to serious emotional distress, which can be magnified by the number of people affected. Traditionally, the right of free speech, at least in the United States, has been regarded as nearly absolute, admitting of exceptions only in cases such as the deliberate provocation of violence, and definitely not in cases of significant yet ephemeral harm—precisely because this is one of the considerations for which the right is considered so important.[4] Even though speech may cause significant harm, it is regarded as important enough in a free society that we protect it despite the harm it may create. Recently, however, the right of free speech has been challenged on exactly such grounds; for instance, there has been a rise in calls for "deplatforming" of offensive speakers, citing the harm they inflict on targeted communities, often challenging their very personhood and right to exist. Although these pleas are rarely made to the government itself, which is the only party that can violate the guarantee of free speech in the First Amendment, the spirit of these limits on speech is consistent with a more nuanced view of that guarantee that displays a greater willingness to compromise it in the face of significant harm (which itself has only come to be appreciated in recent years).[5]

Rights are often thought of as simple and straightforward—and just as often dismissed for the same reasons. It is all too easy to assert a right to something you feel you deserve, but much more difficult to define it, much less defend it by citing a more essential principle that backs it up. However, as we see with free speech, which is considered a very important right that nonetheless admits of exceptions, a statement of a right is just the beginning of a long and detailed discussion. For another example, consider the First Amendment clauses covering the establishment and free exercise of religion in the United States, about which the simple phrase "separation of church and state" obscures a deep and complex history of conflicting rights.[6] In the United States, the Supreme Court and federal appeals courts spend a great deal of time defining, refining, and sometimes overturning rights which, in their original language, every schoolchild and applicant for citizenship learns as if it were a clear and obvious concept.

Typically, we understand rights like these to be based on moral and legal principles embedded in our political and legal system. In the United States, the Declaration of Independence emphasizes the "unalienable rights" of "life, liberty, and the pursuit of happiness," which together with principles of justice and equality also inform the more specific rights spelled out in the Constitution and its amendments. The same holds for the individual rights embedded in documents such as the Magna Carta, the Petition of Rights, and the English Bill of Rights in the United Kingdom, as well as the Declaration of the Rights of Man and of the Citizen in France, which explicitly cites the principles of "liberty, property, security, and resistance to oppression." Although our understanding of these rights may change over time—as does our understanding of the basic moral principles on which they are based—a liberal society's devotion to these rights is foundational, and they should not be subject to democratic vote. Unlike policy decisions that can legitimately change over time as the preferences and priorities of the population changes, these timeless ideals are not properly subject to the same changes. Authority over basic rights is typically reserved for the judges, who are—in theory, at least—insulated from political influence.[7]

This may sound absurd on its face: why, in a democracy, should we remove any issue from the democratic process itself? The answer is that rights are meant to protect everybody, while the democratic process responds to the will of the majority only. If voters are allowed to express preferences over the application and reach of important principles, a majority could vote, through legitimate democratic processes, to deprive a minority of essential rights. Philosopher John Stuart Mill called this a *tyranny of the majority*, explaining that "the 'people' who exercise the power are not always the same people with those over whom it is exercised; and the 'self-government' spoken of is not the government of each by himself, but of each by all the rest."[8] Even though the process by which this happens may be democratic, reflecting the will of the majority, the rights affected should be guaranteed to everyone regardless of the preferences of some. In other words, as paradoxical as it may seem, the defining principles of a democracy are too important to be left to democratic vote.[9]

Mill's concept of the tyranny of the majority provides another way to understand the rights guaranteed in individuals in the amendments to the U.S. Constitution. We don't have to use our imaginations to envision a large group of citizens wanting to limit the speech, association, or religious rights of smaller groups with whom they disagree. This danger applies not just to historically persecuted minorities, such as women, people of color, and LGBTQ+ persons, but anyone who finds themselves in the numerical minority on an issue, who can find their valued rights challenged for what are essentially utilitarian reasons: the harm, distress, or discomfort their beliefs or actions provoke in members of the majority. (As we'll see in Chapter 7, this concept also has relevance to antitrust.)

Although everyone agrees that basic rights should be protected to some extent, we do not necessarily agree on which rights deserve this respect, or which rights are more important than others. This is most visible across the political spectrum, where people on the left and right place different emphasis on particular rights. Generally speaking, traditional liberals focus on rights protecting behavior that is considered more personal, with a prominent example being sexual behavior and freedom, which conservatives are more likely to regulate, control, or ban. By the same token, traditional conservatives focus on commercial or economic rights, valuing the free market—and the interests of business owners that most directly benefit from it—whereas liberals are more likely to restrain the rights of business in the interests of consumers or workers.[10] This dichotomy stems in part from the distinction between "civil rights" and "economic rights," which I shall argue in Chapter 7 is illusory: *all* rights of individuals are personal rights, whether they protect choices made in the bedroom or the boardroom, and regardless of whether those choices are made in a marketplace or not.

PROPERTY RIGHTS

As we saw in Chapter 3, economists and utilitarians in general usually recognize only those rights that are justified by concerns for total welfare or utility.[11] John Stuart Mill wrote eloquently about individual rights and freedoms (especially regarding free speech and thought) in his book *On Liberty*, but ultimately defended these rights on utilitarian grounds, believing them to be essential for a flourishing society.[12] Similarly, economists typically maintain strong support for rights of property and contract, not because they are important in and of themselves in moral terms, but because they contribute to a functioning and prosperous market: after all, nobody can participate in a market without at least a rudimentary concept of property rights (if not contract rights in the case of exchange over time). The contingent way that economists support these rights, however, implies that they will also set them aside if their contribution to prosperity is compromised, such as they do in the case of antitrust law. When confronted with rights grounded in principle rather than utility, some economists are prone to dismiss them as the result of an "arbitrary initial assignment" because they fail to recognize any basis for rights outside of utilitarianism.[13] But rights are not "arbitrarily assigned" if they are based on essential principles that are rooted in the legal and political history of a society—and in liberal societies, these principles support the freedom to choose your own actions within a sphere of autonomy, even if they negatively affect the interests of others, provided these actions do not violate anybody else's rights in the process.

The status of rights in general within utilitarian economics and policymaking is an important and mostly neglected topic, even by economists and philosophers. For the purposes of this book, however, I shall focus specifically on property rights because of their importance to business and commerce, and therefore to antitrust. I argue that the most popular understandings of antitrust law, whether economic or populist, betray a complete disregard for the property rights of business owners.

Like my position on rights in general, this argument does not rely on an extreme, absolutist conception of property rights, but rather a common-sense understanding in which they can legitimately be constrained in the face of other important rights, but cannot be set aside for purely consequentialist reasons (outside of catastrophic harm). We can also see the denial of the property rights of firms by antitrust authorities in how they hold business owners responsible for promoting the general welfare instead of their own rights or interests—at the penalty of criminal sanctions, which are traditionally reserved for blatant wrongdoing (as we discuss in Chapter 7). What's more, this is done for purely utilitarian purposes, because there are no countervailing rights (or catastrophic harm) to justify setting aside firms' property rights. As Adi Ayal writes (in the specific context of monopoly), "while consumers are commonly assumed to deserve the fruits of their labors, as well as the fruits of societal economic growth, monopolists are viewed as merely instrumental: means to an end rather than ends in themselves."[14]

For the purposes of my argument, I use a simple and moderate view of property rights that incorporates strong but not absolute guarantees of use, exclusion, and disposition (or transfer), which are limited only by the equally important rights of others. For example, your right of use implies that you can do what you like in your house or backyard as long as you do not violate the rights of your neighbors to do what they like in their space (for example, by playing loud music at 2am). If you rent your home, your right of use may be limited by the property owner, in exercise of *their* rights (hopefully as spelled out in your lease agreement). Your right of exclusion mean that you can prevent your neighbors from entering your house or yard unless they have a previously agreed-upon right (or easement) allowing them to do so, or in the case of an emergency that excuses the trespass (which waives the right of exclusion out of respect for another valuable right). Finally, your right of disposal mean that you can rent some or all of your house and the land under it to someone else, or sell it altogether, within the real estate laws set up to protect the rights of current and prospective property owners. (Naturally, if you rent your home, you have no rights of disposal!) All of these rights are specific to each individual given their unique circumstances, most importantly the rights of those they interact with (such as tenants, landlords, and neighbors in the case of real estate).

There is a healthy and flourishing literature in philosophy, political theory, and law, in which scholars develop and defend elaborate understandings of the nature of property, including its public and private aspects, and the various rights that individuals have to property in different circumstances and when they should be set aside for various reasons.[15] I hope the understanding I use here is simple and general enough to appeal to those who believe in *essentialist* views of property, which derive rights to property from more basic moral principles (such as John Locke's natural law view of first possession), as well as those who consider property rights to be created by the state, often taking the form of "bundles of rights," collections of specific and malleable rights and liberties that are designed by legislators and courts to meet societal goals (including welfare).[16] The essentialist view more easily accommodates the understanding of property rights I have described, but even the more flexible and instrumental modern view would, in most cases, support and include the basic rights and liberties I have specified above—and even when they would not, I argue that the reasons commonly provided in support of antitrust do not justify excluding them from the bundle of rights that firms have.

Although I focus here on rights to property—and a simple conception of them at that—it could be argued that rights of contract are just as important to discussion of commerce and antitrust, especially when we're talking about buying, renting, or selling property (rather than its ownership in general).[17] Certainly there is a strong connection between property law and contract law, but it is important not to conflate them, as explained by legal scholar J. E. Penner:

Because property rights are so often the subject of contracts it is often supposed that property and contract are intrinsically

linked, or that one is the basis of the other. This single misconception has probably done more to confuse the understanding of
both subjects than anything else. The concept of property does
comprise inalienability, but the concept of property does not
depend on the existence of a right to create binding agreements.[18]

He goes on to make clear that property rights and contract rights are
not overlapping, but rather work together:

Now, given the fact that we do have the right to make binding
agreements, it is certainly arguable that we ought to be able to
make binding agreements about licensing or transferring our
property. No aspect of the right of exclusive use indicates that
property right should *not* be the subject of contracts. Even so, the
right to exchange property rights is not entailed by the right of
exclusive use. It arises because we have both property rights and
a generally unlimited right to make contracts.[19]

In other words, property law protects the general rights of owners
to dispose of their property, while contract law covers how that will
happen in the context of voluntary exchange. Having said this, I feel
comfortable in discussing property rights in isolation from contract
rights, relying on Penner's statement earlier in his book that "the right
to transfer property is an inherent feature of property rights."[20]

RIGHTS OF BUSINESS OWNERS

Under this moderate understanding of property rights, we should also
recognize that rights apply not only to individuals acting separately, as
consumers and workers, but also to individuals cooperating in groups,
including in businesses. For the majority of us who are not hermits (or
writers), much of our activity happens together with others, and the
behavior of groups, whether government agencies, community groups,
or business firms, is the expression of the choices of their members (as
combined through collective decision-making procedures). This is not

to dismiss the difficulty with assigning responsibility for the actions of groups to individuals involved in collective decision-making, which has made issues of government accountability and corporate liability very complicated for many years. It is merely to say that groups of individuals, as well as the individuals who make them up, can possess meaningful property rights, which cannot be dismissed for purely welfarist purposes.

Despite the somewhat formal presentation above, this idea that business owners have property rights is not a controversial or radical position. Business owners are commonly understood to be able to provide the goods and services they want, package and promote them however they think will be appealing to their customers, and sell them at the prices and other terms they choose—which their customers are free to accept or reject, in the exercise of their own property rights. Firms can locate (and relocate) where they choose; hire, promote, and dismiss employees within the terms of their contracts and labor laws; and invest in other businesses when they find this financially lucrative. Although we can speak of businesses having and exercising "their" property rights, we really mean the property rights of the owners, which they exercise themselves, or they assign that role to agents or managers (especially in the case of corporations, where this linkage is even less direct). The mechanisms of control and governance may be simple or complicated, but ultimately their foundations rest in the property rights of the owners of the business.

Based on this simple understanding, I maintain that the property rights of firms are morally valid and important, and should be protected as long as they do not use their rights to violate the rights of others (such as engaging in fraudulent or deceitful practices). These rights should be respected regardless of the circumstances in which the business operates, including the nature of their market or industry—even if that firm is a monopoly.

Yes, monopolists have rights too, despite their often being cast as "evil" in popular culture as well as academia and policy circles. As Ayal writes, the rights of monopolists "are almost never discussed," which raises the questions of "what justifies treating them differently from others whose property is protected by the state."[21] The rights of a small pizza shop operating in a large city with hundreds of other pizza shops would not ordinarily be questioned, assuming the shop exercised their rights in a way consistent with the rights of others (and the relevant labor and safety laws). But if we change the example to a firm with little competition, that firm's property rights are significantly curtailed: its actions in exercise of its rights are scrutinized for their effects on total welfare and consumer well-being, and any behavior that is judged to have a negative impact on these measures renders the firm subject to criminal and civil liability. As Ayal writes, "what has become the commonsensical view masks a hidden assumption—that monopolists as such are to be limited unless *others* benefit from their practices."[22] These actions can be the same ones engaged in by a small firm with more competition, but simply because the large firm with less competition will have a larger impact on welfare, their actions become important enough to justify a restriction of property rights and liberties—all in the name of the same utilitarian measures that rights were instituted to protect firms against. To quote Ayal once more, "were efficiency-maximizing rules to be applied in other contexts as they are in antitrust, we would have a rebellion on our hands by those claiming infringement of their rights to governmental respect of property and freedom of contract."[23]

Although what I present may be a common understanding of property rights in general, it is hardly the common view of the property rights of businesses, especially monopoly and other firms in less competitive industries, against whom antitrust action is regarded by many as just and necessary. As we saw above, Ayal recognizes that monopoly rights are rarely taken seriously; furthermore, the antitrust enforcement that is heralded as "purely economic," which we already saw is misguided on its face, is revealed through adherents' attitudes to have a distinctly moralistic tone: "[A]ntitrust is often associated with criminality, and . . . its enforcement enjoys a huge consensus as to its appropriateness and moral value. Those violating it are not seen merely as harming economic efficiency, but violating moral principles and stealing something that does not belong to them. . . . Monopoly is viewed as inherently unfair, if not outright evil."[24] This leads to a turn-about in which, not only are monopoly rights ignored, but monopoly behavior *per se* becomes subject to challenge and must respond to calls for justification. But as legal philosopher Richard Epstein writes with respect to commerce in general,

> justification presupposes a *prima facie* wrong that stands in need of justification. And what is important is that a system of liberty and private property is able to identify as well those actions that need no justification at all. The social presumption to set in favor of liberty of action, notwithstanding the ownership claims of others. Only force and fraud against person or property upset that presumption.[25]

As stated before and reiterated here by Epstein, the only wrongs that would justify restrictions on the exercise of property rights would be force, fraud, and deceit or misrepresentation, and "it is the absence" of these actions that "defines the very domain of antitrust offenses."[26] Of course, these apply to small firms in competitive industries as well as large firms in concentrated ones, but have little to do with antitrust law as it is enforced, which focuses solely on the effects of firm behavior on overall welfare or consumer well-being, focusing on harm rather than wrongdoing.

In the same spirit, economist Dominick Armentano asserts plainly that

> the antitrust laws, by their very nature, appear to interfere with private property rights. Antitrust prohibition of price discrimination, merging, price fixing, and even free-market monopolization prevents freely contracting parties who hold legitimate rights to property from making, or refusing to make, certain contractual arrangements that they believe to be in their best interests.[27]

What, then, justifies the limitations put on the free exercise of valid property rights of firms by antitrust? The obvious answer would be the equally valid rights of consumers and other competitors, but these are much more difficult to identify.

RIGHTS OF CONSUMERS

In most understandings (including both economic and populist), antitrust protects other parties from harm due to the action of offending firms. As I said in Chapter 1, anticompetitive behavior clearly causes harm, but we should also acknowledge that a lot of behavior creates harm without being wrongful or violating any rights. If I stop shopping at a local store, I harm the interests of the owners; if I quit my job, I harm the interests of my employers; and if a business closes, it harms the interests of its customers and employees. Although they are all harmful, none of these actions would be considered wrongful because no rights were violated. All of these actions are expressions of valid rights, either mine as a consumer or worker or the business owner's property rights, in the same way that disturbing speech is an exercise of the speaker's rights. (We'll discuss harm and wrong more generally in Chapter 6.)

Of course, antitrust law is not concerned with one business closing, raising its prices, or changing its product line—unless it is large and influential enough that these actions have an impact on the rest of the industry and its consumers. Antitrust focuses on actions that threaten to lessen the degree of competition in a market enough that consumer surplus or overall welfare could be significantly affected. But the principle is the same: regardless of the degree of harm seen or anticipated, what rights are violated by anticompetitive behavior that justifies the limitation of business owners' property rights?

The obvious answer would seem to be the rights of consumers and other firms, who are the prime beneficiaries of antitrust law. If anyone's rights are violated by anticompetitive behavior, it would be the parties who suffer harm from it. However, although their interests are clearly affected, it is difficult to imagine what rights consumers or competitors have to particular behavior from firms or certain market outcomes in general.

For now, let's focus on consumers.[28] (We'll look more at the rights of other competitors in the Chapter 5 in the context of specific antitrust violations.) After all, each of us is a consumer, whatever other roles we play in the economy, so we all have a stake in this discussion. As consumers, we are harmed when prices increase, which is the most direct impact of anticompetitive behavior. Either we pay more for a product we need and have less money to spend on other goods and services (or devote to other purposes, such as savings or philanthropy), or we buy less of the more expensive product than we planned (and wanted), or we have to switch to a less-preferred alternative—or, failing that, go without it altogether. Obviously this harm is greater the more necessary a purchase is or how few substitutes there are, medication and gasoline being two prime examples, but there is some harm done whenever the price of a good or service rises, as we know from personal experience as well as the welfare economics surveyed in Chapter 2.

According to antitrust scholar Herbert Hovenkamp, "few people dispute that antitrust's core mission is protecting *consumers' rights* to the low prices, innovation, and diverse production that competition promises."[29] But the imposition of harm does not mean that rights were violated—or that they even exist. Do consumers have a right to low prices (aside from whatever right is implied by antitrust law itself)? We have to imagine how such a right would be defined. Do consumers have a right to whatever the current price is, and increases in the price violate this right? Or do they have a right to the price that would result from the conditions of perfect competition, which is usually understood to equal the marginal cost of production? Perhaps the right is defined in more of a "fuzzy" way, and it is violated only if the price rises above a certain threshold level above one of the prices suggested here. Of course, prices in general rise over time due to inflation, so maybe consumers have a right to the price of a certain item increasing no faster than the inflation rate, or at least not much faster. But what if the product changes? Companies improve products all the time, often resulting in a higher price—and they just as often reduce size while keeping the price the same (which, when the practice is widespread, is known as *shrink-flation*). Do consumers have a right against this?

This only scratches the surface of all the questions that are raised by the possibility of a right on the part of consumers to a certain price. But this exercise was rather facetious, because no such right is recognized in any society with anything resembling a free-market economy. It could be said to be implied by legal restrictions on prices, such as rent control and caps on the costs of prescription drugs, but these laws are normally justified by citing the catastrophic harm caused by market forces in particular situations, not a general right to low prices on the part of consumers. Other rights are sometimes invoked on the parts of citizens, such as rights to housing and healthcare, but these would support public provision or funding of such services rather than a certain price at which they would be offered. One could interpret these rights to be, effectively, rights to a price of zero, but that would be obscuring the point of these rights (where and when they are maintained).

For most goods and services in a moderately free-market economy, consumers are not understood to have any right to a certain price, any more than they have a right to a certain assortment of products, a certain location of businesses, or a certain number of business from which to choose. As Armentano writes, "such private activities such as price discrimination, merging, tying, and price fixing appear to violate no property rights in the ordinary sense of the term; that is, they do not necessarily involve force, fraud, or misrepresentation."[30] If they did have such rights, it would apply to all firms regardless of their size or the nature of their industry; your neighborhood bakery as well as national chains would be prohibited from raising the price of donuts, removing a favorite donut from the offerings, or closing a location. Larger firms facing less competition do more harm with these actions than small firms do, but the violation of such a right on the part of consumers would be the same—all firms would be acting wrongfully if they acted to raise prices if consumers had a right protecting them from this.

More generally, consumers do not have a right to any particular outcome from a market process, whether this is the result of one large firm's actions or those of many small firms. Consumers do have the right to honest dealings, voluntary market transactions free of fraud and deceit in which they receive what they paid for. They may think the price they pay is too high, or the size and the quality of the product they receive too low, and that they got more value for their money in the past. (They also earned less money in the past, but that's inflation again.) They have the option to switch products or sellers, boycott the company, or start an online protest; all of these choices are completely within the consumer's property rights, just as setting the sale price is within the property rights of the seller. But consumers have no right to a certain price, much less one that is enforceable by law—or one that justifies the limitation of the property rights of business owners.

Another way to think of a "right" on the part of consumers to a certain price is that sellers who charge a higher price would be wrongfully taking property that belongs to consumers. In other words, some regard the transfer of surplus from consumers to sellers that results from an increase in price, or prices set above the perfectly competitive level, as theft. This is how this is interpreted by some antitrust advocates, such as Robert H. Lande, who writes that "the overriding purpose of the antitrust statutes is to prevent firms from stealing from consumers by charging them supracompetitive prices. When firms use their market power to raise prices to supracompetitive levels, consumers pay more for their goods and services, and these overcharges constitute a taking of consumers' property."[31] At the end of his article, Lande puts it more plainly: "We could politely call this a concern with the wealth transfer effects of market power. Or we could bluntly, but accurately, characterize these as situations where the firms are stealing from consumers."[32]

What's more, Lande finds such thinking in the original debates over the Sherman Act, the first major piece of antitrust legislation in the United States, with senators (including John Sherman himself) using terms such as "robbery" and "extortion" to refer to the actions of trusts, cartels, and monopolists.[33] On this basis, Lande asks if, perhaps, "Congress in effect awarded the property right to what we today call 'consumers' surplus' to consumers?"[34] Lande's analysis is curiously parallel to mine: he is arguing that the traditional economic focus of antitrust obscures the moral wrong of theft at its heart, while I argue that it obscures the moral wrong done to producers. The difference is that we find the relevant rights in different places: he finds them in the hands of consumers, which has no basis in traditional conceptions of property rights but only in the Sherman Act itself, whereas I find them in the traditionally recognized property rights of business owners.

Others agree that price increases may involve theft. In the context of collusion, Alex Raskolnikov writes that the cooperating firms "in essence transfer money from consumers to themselves. This is done intentionally (that is, with an intent to benefit from collusively set prices). And consumers surely do not consent to being *fleeced*."[35] On the same topic, Judy Whalley, an attorney with the US Department of Justice, wrote: "These clandestine, collusive practices constitute no more than fraud and theft from consumers. There can be no doubt that price-fixing in all its forms is a serious crime. It cannot be inadvertently committed, it causes substantial social harm including distortion of the proper allocation of resources, and it creates no redeeming social benefits."[36] Note that Whalley associates the category of crime with "substantial social harm" with "no redeeming social benefits," a utilitarian understanding of wrongdoing that does not recognize any role for rights (which will be discussed further in Chapter 6).

The allegation that price increases represent not only harm to consumers—which is undeniable, just as price decreases harm sellers—but wrongful theft from them, is problematic in several ways. First, it begs the question of exactly what claim consumers have to a certain level of prices, which takes us back to the issue of whether such a right exists; after all, if consumer surplus is property that can be stolen, there must be a recognized right protecting it. What's more, Lande refers specifically to supracompetitive prices, or prices in excess of the perfectly competitive level (where they equal marginal cost), which is impossible to reach in the real world, rendering it a purely hypothetical or counterfactual notion that holds real-world firms to an unreasonable standard. In general, the basis for this argument is the idea of the "just price," which maintains the existence of a fair or ethical price based on essential worth, value, or cost.[37] This concept has its origins in ancient philosophy, theology, and classical economics, and was supplanted largely by modern subjectivist understandings of value (especially in economics), although it was reflected in a 1923 United States Supreme Court case that claimed the consumer is "morally entitled to obtain the worth of his money," and has been revived in Neo-Brandeisian arguments for the use of antitrust to generate "fair" outcomes (on which more later).[38]

Finally, if simply setting price above marginal cost represents theft from consumers, then *any* firm that charges prices over cost—which is to say every real-world firm—is guilty, regardless of any evidence or suspicion of collusion with other firms or other attempts to lessen competition. In general, when a seller raises the price for a good or service it is offering for sale, a price that can be accepted, rejected, or negotiated down by a buyer, it is merely participating in the process of voluntary exchange, and does not come close to theft unless the seller is deceitful about some aspect of the product itself, which is not a matter for antitrust as usually considered. Although the allegation that high prices constitute theft may seem extreme, it does provide a fine example of the tendency of antitrust advocates, like economists and utilitarians in general, to conflate the ideas of harm and wrong, a topic we shall explore at more length in Chapter 6.

Having laid out the conception of rights, and property rights in particular, we are now ready to apply them to the traditional violations of antitrust law: price collusion, merger, and exclusionary practices. We covered the simple economic logic behind these prohibitions in Chapter 2, but in the next chapter we'll see how this story changes when the property rights of business owners are recognized—and violations of anyone else's rights are hard to find.

5

Antitrust violations and rights

Much of our discussion to this point has been fairly abstract—especially for a book about antitrust and competition law, which would usually be consumed with the fine minutiae of legislative politics, corporate history, and judicial opinions. So it might be helpful at this point to look at how the philosophical conception of rights that we outlined in Chapter 4 apply to the most significant violations of antitrust or competition law, allowing us to see how a rights-focused approach differs from the standard economic one (and the Neo-Brandeisian one when appropriate).

COLLUSION AND PRICE-FIXING

Let's start with what is probably the most obvious antitrust violation: collusive price-fixing. Firms cannot, by law, conspire to maintain prices above where they would if the firms set them independently and competitively. Even in industries that are less competitive to begin with, in which firms earn significant profits, they can increase their total profits by collectively agreeing to raise their prices. In effect, they would be acting as if they were a monopoly, splitting its higher profit among different divisions or departments. If successful, the higher prices lower output and consumer surplus, and despite the higher profits, total welfare falls, as we saw in Chapter 2. There is nothing special or unique about price-fixing: any instance of collusion between firms competing in the same industry is considered anticompetitive and therefore potentially illegal. But price-fixing is most clearly and directly related to consumer surplus and overall welfare, given the role that prices play in the market analysis.

If we look at price-fixing from the perspective of rights, however, the matter becomes much less clear and hardly obvious. The rights of disposal included in most common-sense conceptions of property rights would include the right to set the terms at which a seller offers a good or service. Firms are free to lower or raise their price as they choose, and consumers are free to respond by buying more or less as they choose. Consumers have the right to use their resources to make the purchases they want, and can accept or reject the offers made by sellers, but they have no right to a particular price (absent a previous guarantee or contract from the seller, such as a raincheck).

The difference with collusive price-fixing, of course, is that firms are no longer setting their prices independently of each other. Instead of competing, which results in lower prices, they are cooperating, which results in higher prices (and lower consumer surplus and total welfare). If one firm in an industry raises its price alone, it loses some business to its competitors, but if many or all firms in an industry raise their prices together, consumers have fewer alternatives (other than seeking out a substitute product from firms in another industry). Even if the firms together lose some business due to higher prices, they will more than likely make up the revenue due to the higher price, because they are starting from a relatively competitive price and would need to raise it a lot before they would reach the profit-maximizing monopoly price.

Consumers are hurt whenever any firm raises it price, and they are hurt more when many firms raise prices together. But are their rights violated when firms collude to raise prices? Even if we accept, following the discussion in Chapter 4, that consumers have no rights to certain levels of prices, so they are not wrongfully affected when one firm raises it price, does this change when two or more firms raise their prices together? Do consumers have a right against price increases from more than one firm at the same time?

This wouldn't seem to make sense either, because all the firms in an industry can raise their prices at the same time for reasons other than collusion. Firms who produce a similar good or service rely on the same inputs, such as labor, land, and raw materials. For example, many food manufacturers use wheat and eggs, both of which, at the time of writing this book, are much more expensive due to events beyond firms' control, but nonetheless drive up the overall price level of food. Automotive manufacturers use steel and rubber, the prices of which fluctuate regularly and affect the prices of cars and trucks. And the price of gasoline affects the price of anything that must be transported, usually in tandem (and therefore contributing to overall inflation).

No one would claim that the rights of consumers are violated when one firm raises its price (for whatever reason), nor would anyone make such a claim when multiple firms in an industry raise their prices for a reason such as a shared increase in costs. What exactly, then, is the right of consumer that is violated when multiple firms raise their prices due to an agreement between them? Do consumers have a right to the absence of collusion? That would be a very specific right to declare and defend on the part of consumers, and suffice it to say it has never been recognized as such. Of course, collusion among firms to fix prices can be (and usually is) considered a criminal conspiracy, but this begs the question of identifying the wrongful activity at the heart of the "conspiracy," bringing us back to the question of what right of consumers is violated by a firm raising its price (or several firms doing so together).

However, if we think of this in a different way, it becomes more palatable: perhaps consumers have a right to competition itself, specifically between firms in the same industry. This would explain the fact that firms responding in parallel to a shared increase in costs doesn't raise concern: it's simply an outcome of the competitive process that helps keep the firms in business (unless enough consumers respond to the higher prices by shifting to the product of another industry). If cookie manufacturers all raise their prices in response to an increase in the price of wheat, that's the result of each firm adjusting their production and sales strategies to accommodate a new cost environment. Because the increase in the price of wheat affects all the cookie manufacturers at the same time, their prices rise together, but as the result of competition, not the suppression of it.

Furthermore, this has a different effect on firms: the cookie manufacturers have passed some of their cost increase on to consumers, reducing their consumer surplus, but their profits fall at the same time, given the increase in costs and the fall in demand they will experience. Total welfare in the market for cookies falls, but as the result of an external "supply shock," not a lapse in competition. If those same cookie manufacturers instead conspire to raise their prices, in the absence of any external cost increase, for no reason other than to increase their profits, the resulting industry-wide price increase is due to a decline in competition. Those firms have chosen *not* to compete, but instead to cooperate—as we said before, to attempt to behave as a monopoly rather than as a number of separate firms, and thereby raise all of their profits.

Do consumers have a right to a competitive market? As legal scholar Alan Meese tells us, this was essentially the position of the courts in the early days of antitrust, according to whom "the state could only outlaw contracts whose primary effect was to restrain liberty in a manner that led to prices higher than those that would otherwise be produced by the 'natural' state of economic affairs, that is, a competitive market with no barriers to entry."[1] A competitive market is in the interests of consumers, of course, just as collusion is in the interests of the firms. A competitive market is also in the interests of society overall, in the sense that it increases total welfare. But something merely being in someone's interests doesn't imply, as the courts mentioned above, that they have a right to it. Think about what this would mean: consumers would have a right to a certain mode of operation on the part of all the firms from whom they buy goods and services. Stated this way, we see that such a right is not to the presence of competition itself, but to independent decision-making among firms, regardless of what degree of competition results from it (which depends on many factors external to the choices of the firms themselves). This right would prohibit cooperative behavior among firms to maximize their joint profits, especially if it results to higher prices, but would allow for independent profit-maximization on the part of each firm—even if it results in higher prices.

Following this logic, the rights of consumers don't have anything to do with prices at all, but rather the process by which they are chosen.

This makes more sense of the claims of "theft" discussed in Chapter 4, especially if we maintain that anticompetitive behavior such as collusion is not just harmful but wrong as well. If we believe that cooperation between firms is wrongful, because it violates the rights of consumers to a competitive market, then the results of cooperation—higher prices and lower consumer surplus—could be seen as wrongful as well, taking something that consumers are entitled to have and keep.

Although they don't use the terms of rights, antitrust advocates do effectively endorse a right of consumers to independent business operation when they hold up competition as the most important aspect of the market economy, which we shall discuss in Chapter 8. For now, we need to turn back to the right itself and try to find an independent moral basis for it, grounded in basic principles or more essential rights, not mere (non-catastrophic) negative consequences.

Perhaps we could say that this right is based on the moral prohibition against fraud and deceit, which, as we saw earlier, results from the basic respect owed all persons. No business has the right to lie to consumers about the product they are selling, or to sell a fraudulent product (which reflects an implicit lie about its quality or characteristics). In other words, firms have a duty to abstain from fraud or deceit, which implies a right of consumers not to be cheated or lied to. Firms are free to use their property rights however they choose as long as they don't violate the rights of consumers, and fraudulent or deceitful behavior does exactly that.

Does this apply to collusion or cooperation as well? Fraud or deceit on the part of businesses usually applies to the goods and services they offer or the terms of the offer itself, not the decision-making processes that led to them. Firms don't usually make statements or promises of independent decision-making to consumers, which would then become false in the presence of collusion. (They may make such statements to antitrust enforcers in defense against an accusation, but that's in the context of such behavior being declared illegal.) It is difficult to argue that cooperative behavior among firms in the same industry represents any sort of dishonesty on their parts, given they rarely make claims to the contrary.

Another way to argue for a right of consumers to independent behavior of the part of firms is to appeal to fairness. After all, isn't it obviously unfair for firms to collude on the terms they offer consumers for their goods and services? This may sound obvious, but the meaning of the word "fairness" is doing a lot of work here. Fairness is a notoriously vague concept, which in the worst case can become, as economically-oriented antitrust scholars Phillip Areeda and Donald Turner famously put it, a "vagrant claim applied to any value that one happens to favor."[2] In philosophy and law, however, it usually comes down to equal or just treatment, what Aristotle described as "treating like cases alike."[3] For example, a game is considered fair if the rules are applied to everyone equally and not set aside or ignored out of preference for a certain competitor; the same goes for the concept of "the rule of law" in a democracy, which holds elected leaders to the same legal expectations as "ordinary" citizens.[4]

We usually say fairness means that rules and laws are applied equally, but we use it less often to describe the nature and content of the rules and laws themselves—unless it can be shown that they were designed to give some undeserved advantage over others, which would be considered unfair under the more general rules or laws governing how specific rules or laws are made. In other words, fairness is usually defined by more precise concepts of equality and justice (which for this reason are more commonly used terms in philosophy). When you judge a practice or outcome to be unfair, you need to say more precisely what you mean by "unfair," which usually demands an explanation as to why it treats people unequally or unjustly.

So, does collusion among firms in an industry imply that they treat consumers unequally or unjustly? If by "unequally" we mean that some consumers are treated better than others, then no, assuming all consumers pay the same higher price that results from collusion. (When different groups of consumers pay different prices, this is called *price discrimination*, which is a separate practice that can nonetheless invoke discussions of fairness as well as antitrust attention if its use is explicitly anticompetitive.)[5] Perhaps we mean that consumers are treated unequally compared to the firms themselves, but this makes little sense, given their separate and opposite roles in the market process. Finally, accusations of unjust treatment (or injustice) bring us back to the issue of whether rights are violated—but that's the question we're trying to answer, so that's no help.

If industry collusion seems unfair to consumers, it is more likely based on the harm it does to them, which again is undeniable but is not wrongful if no rights can be found to be violated. By the same token, increased competition in an industry can be considered unfair to the firms in it—especially those which are forced out of business due to a combination of lower prices and less efficiency than other competitors—but this does not violate the rights of any of them.

MERGER

The same logic we applied to collusive price-fixing also applies to mergers between firms competing in the same industry, or *horizontal mergers* (as opposed to *vertical mergers*, which occur between firms at different levels of production, such as manufacturing and distribution or whole-sale and retail, as discussed in Chapter 2). Merger can be considered a way for firms to formalize and legitimize their cooperation: rather than trying to coordinate decisions between two managerial structures, which may be cumbersome or difficult even if it weren't illegal, the two firms can merge into one, with one unified managerial structure making decisions on what to do with their combined assets.

Whereas price-fixing is absolutely (or *per se*) forbidden under antitrust or competition law, being regarded as a clearly anticompetitive action with obvious harms and no offsetting benefit to welfare, merger is normally challenged only in cases where the negative impact on consumer surplus or welfare is predicted to be significant (according to the *rule of reason*).[6] A merger between the smallest two firms out of five, or the largest two out of ten, may not be grounds for critical attention, but a merger between the largest two firms out of five likely would be. Only the latter merger would be expected to reduce competition in the industry significantly enough to raise price and lower consumer surplus and welfare enough to justify investigation.

Furthermore, unlike collusion where firms remain separate, mergers that result in a new firm structure are often defended on grounds of increased efficiency. A merged manufacturing company producing the output of two firms may need to retain most of the productive capacity of the original firms, but perhaps not all of their managerial staff, human resources personnel, marketing teams, and so forth. In addition, the larger firm may be able to negotiate better terms on inputs such as raw materials, leasing costs, and real estate, further lowering its costs compared to the original firms. These increased efficiencies would enable the merged firm to be more competitive in the industry, potentially using its lower costs to undercut the prices of its competitors. Of course, the new firm may also keep prices the same and enjoy the higher profits margins, but this would imply unrealized profits which would make the firm ripe for a takeover attempt. In either case, the increased efficiency of the new merged firm would offset, to some extent, the natural tendency for prices to rise in the face of reduced competition, lessening the negative impact of the merger on consumer surplus and welfare (and possibly increasing them).

Compared to the *per se* illegality of price-fixing, horizontal merger has more ambiguous consequences based on a number of factors including the nature of the relevant industry and the efficiency implications of the merger. Due to this, antitrust authorities typically take these factors (and many more) into account when assessing a planned merger for possible legal or regulatory action.[7] Although this sounds reasonable, it also highlights the purely consequentialist nature of antitrust and competition law, by which actions on the part of firms are questioned only if they have a substantially negative effect on consumer surplus or welfare. Even though price-fixing violates no recognized rights of consumers, it is treated as a wrong and penalized regardless of the realized effects on consumers—the conspiracy to collude is itself the crime. But merger itself is not held to be wrong *per se*, although it will be prevented or penalized if it is found to lower welfare sufficiently. This reveals merger to be regarded as wrong, not by definition, but only if it fails to promote the common good—which is normally not considered the responsibility of private parties, even if they happen to run a business.

Considered from the viewpoint of basic property rights, even this conditional scrutiny of merger is difficult to justify. The standard right of disposal would normally be understood to include the right to sell the assets of a company to another (whether an existing competitor or a new entity absorbing both). The final outcome of a merger could be achieved by other means that would presumably raise no questions from antitrust authorities. For example, one firm could, over time, grow to the size of two, while another could shrink and eventually fail; alternatively, the second firm could go out of business for some other reason and sell its assets to the first. But the act of merger in particular arouses enforcement attention, especially if the intent is suspected to be similar to that behind price-fixing. However, intent is irrelevant to a valid exercise of basic property rights that violates no rights of others.

We should not gloss over this possibility, though. Does merger violate any other party's rights? The answer with respect to consumers would seem similar to when we were discussing their rights in the context of price-fixing: unless there is a moral principle that would support a right to a certain number of firms in an industry, consumers have no right that is violated by merger. (Even if the merger raises the prices of goods and services in its industry, that still violates no right, as discussed earlier.)

However, there are also the merged firm's other competitors in the industry to consider. Do they have rights that are violated by a merger in their industry? Although the Neo-Brandeisians and their forebears who wrote the original antitrust legislation were concerned with both consumers and competitors (especially smaller, less efficient ones), economic conceptions of antitrust pay less attention to the well-being of other firms. Their focus on consumer surplus and welfare makes them less sympathetic to higher-cost firms whose existence may be threatened by an efficiency-enhancing merger; such a merger increases competition in the sense that it makes it harder for less efficient firms to survive. However, the failure of less efficient firms also reduces the number of firms in an industry, making it less competitive in the long run. (We'll see a similar process play out when we discuss predatory pricing below.)

Assuming they are not driven out of business, other firms facing a merger in their industry will nonetheless experience ambiguous effects. On the one hand, they benefit from any price increases, in the sense that any reduction in competition brings the industry closer to monopoly, with its higher total profits representing a rising tide that lifts all ships. (These higher prices will also attract new firms into the industry, which would restore some of the competition lessened by the merger, bringing prices back down a bit.) On the other hand, any increased efficiencies the new firm gains will make it a more formidable competitor, enabling them to grab up more market share and limit any price increases that were the silver lining in this situation. But even if other competitors see their profits fall after the merger, this does not imply the existence of a right against merger.

In fact, the mere suggestion that one firm has a right to limit the behavior of a competitor is odd, given the extremely limited nature of their interactions. Firms who produce and sell goods and services engage in transactions with consumers, not with other firms that produce similar products. (Firms do engage with other firms at different levels of production, but in this sense the firms purchasing goods and services from another firm is in the role of a consumer, not a competitor.) After all, we expect competitors to compete, and any actions on the part of one firm that have a negative impact on another—such as lowering their price—is usually regarded as a pro-competitive act that increases consumer surplus and welfare. Of course, firms have rights against fraud and deceit on the part of their competitors, such as when one firm lies to consumers about the quality of another firm's products; both consumers and competitors have a legitimate and recognized right against this. But firms do not have a right against standard exercises of property rights that, through the process of competition, lower their profits (just as consumers have no rights against actions that lower their surplus).

EXCLUSIONARY PRACTICES

However, there are actions a firm can take that are not addressed to its consumers but rather to its competitors, which are regarded as anti-competitive in nature. These are often called *exclusionary practices*, and they include any actions of one firm (or several firms in collusion) that are meant to limit the commercial opportunities of another firm, such as exclusive contracts (including vertical mergers), tying arrangements, and predatory pricing (which we discuss at length below).[8]

A sports analogy may help: in American football, when the quarterback throws the ball to a receiver, players on the other team can try to catch it, but they're not allowed to push the receiver so they cannot catch it (which results in a penalty called pass interference). You can also think of two managers going for the same promotion: ideally, each candidate would demonstrate to their boss how much they can contribute to the firm in the new role, but it defeats the purpose for them to devote their time instead to attacking each other. (Unfortunately, political candidates are rarely held to this standard.)

In the same spirit, firms are encouraged to compete for consumers' business by offering a better product, lower price, and other attractive terms, but not to interfere, directly or indirectly, with how other firms do business. Unlike "normal" competitive behavior, which reduces prices and benefits consumers, firms engaging in exclusionary practices sometimes use means other than standard commerce to limit the output of their competitors, or the number of competitors at all, which has the opposite effects. Other times, they use the usual means of commerce, like lowering prices, as a long-term strategy to exact more permanent injury on their competitors.

Like collusion and merger, exclusionary practices are yet another way for firms in industries with some degree of competition to approach or simulate a state of monopoly, in the hope of acquiring the higher total profits that come with it. Unlike collusion and merger, which reflect cooperation between firms, exclusionary practices represent conflict between them, in which "a firm having a monopoly position invests some of its monopoly profits in making it unprofitable for others to complete with it, thus perpetuating its monopoly."[9]

The effects on consumer surplus and welfare of some exclusionary practices are not so clear, however, especially if they take place over time and, at least for a while, they involve behavior that seems to be directed at consumers—and in a way that benefits them. Perhaps the most interesting and controversial example is predatory pricing.[10] The typical scenario starts with a large dominant firm facing competition from small upstarts. (Imagine a large department store chain and smaller independent store serving the same downtown area, or a large airline competing against smaller airlines in the same airport.) If the large firm is more efficient than the smaller firms, or has more cash reserves or access to financing, it can lower its price enough to drive the smaller firms out of business (or at least out of that particular market). After the smaller firms close or move, the large firm can then raise its price again, at least until a new upstart firm tries to enter its market.

Scholars have identified a number of practical problems with this story, but I'll mention just two. First, although in the long run predatory pricing serves to reinforce high prices and keeps consumer surplus down, it does benefit consumers in the short run—which may be a significant period of time, depending on how long the smaller firms can stick it out. (They may be able to attract short-term financing if there is hope of winning the game of chicken against the larger firm, who despite their more secure financial position is still losing money.) And if entry into the market is relatively low-cost, it may not take long for a new entrant to replace the failed one, starting the process anew, which benefits consumers and society as a whole. (Entrepreneurs are optimistic by nature, remember.)

If this happens often enough, the dominant firm may have incentive to keep its prices low more regularly—perhaps not as low as when it's trying to drive smaller firms out of its market, but low enough to deter new entrants. In certain instances, this threat of potential competition can prevent a dominant firm (or even a monopolist) from raising prices as high as it would like, limiting its negative effect on consumer surplus and total welfare. Even if it only happens once, and the dominant firm is able to fend off the new competitor and restore its original price, consumers are no worse off in the long run—and they may be significantly better off during the period of intense price competition. The only sense in which they are worse off is compared to the hypothetical situation in which the dominant firm accepts and accommodates the smaller competitor, resulting in lower prices over the long term (but not as low in the short term), which is the standard justification based on consumer surplus and welfare for prohibiting predatory pricing.

Second, predatory pricing is simple to explain in theory, and almost as easy to diagnose in the real world after the fact, once the smaller competitors have been driven out and prices return to their higher level. However, it is very difficult to detect and confirm as it is happening, because the only visible change is lower prices, which are usually considered by the antitrust authorities (and economists in general) to be a good thing.[11] Furthermore, price competition is *supposed* to weed out less efficient firms, so even when smaller upstarts leave the market, this is not necessarily a sign of anything wrong. To the contrary, it could be a sign that competition is working, not being thwarted. While the intense price competition is happening, authorities may reasonably suspect, based on the structure of the market and the relative size of the firms within it, that such price cuts are strategic in nature, but there is no way to be sure—and even if there were, they might not want to charge a firm with illegal behavior while it is currently benefiting consumers with lower prices.

It is only after the less efficient firms drop out of the market and the dominant firm can once again raise its price is there any evidence that the earlier decrease in price was not simply intended to gain market share from its competitors, but to drive them out altogether (especially if the price was so low as to endanger the dominant firm's profits as well). Such evidence may seem cut and dried if not for the fact that firms raise prices for many reasons: costs rise, products are improved, and consumer demand changes, not to mention the competitive actions of other firms in the industry that affect each other (including the emergence of a new competitor to take the place of the old one). The antitrust authorities are aware of all of this, of course, and they scrutinize these possibilities (and many more) in an attempt to discover or rule out alternative explanations for the increase in price.[12]

In general, predatory pricing serves an example of how difficult it can be to determine whether a given action on the part of a firm increases or decreases competition (and in which way). In a paper examining the real-world effects of antitrust enforcement on consumer surplus, economists Robert Crandall and Clifford Winston explain that the economic theory of antitrust

> has proven remarkably fertile in pointing out how various actions by firms may be interpreted as either procompetitive or anti-competitive. For example, when prices decline sufficiently so that no firm in an industry is earning economic profits and some firms exit, this outcome may reflect a highly competitive market adjusting to a condition of temporary oversupply, or it could indicate that a large competitor is employing a strategy of predatory pricing to drive out its rivals. Similarly, when a firm builds a large factory, it may be engaged in vigorous competition and new entry, or it may be creating excess capacity as an implicit threat to potential competitors that it may raise output and cut price quickly if circumstances warrant. Although economic theory can help organize analysis of the economic variables affected by antitrust policy, it often offers little policy guidance because almost any action by a firm short of outright price fixing can turn out to have procompetitive or anticompetitive consequences.[13]

The fact that antitrust has difficulty identifying particular examples of firm behavior as either procompetitive or anticompetitive does not just emphasize the complexity of the required welfare analysis (at which economists are experts), but also several aspects of antitrust that are more general. First, whether behavior is judged to be procompetitive or anticompetitive by antitrust authorities has nothing to do with the process of competition itself but rather the eventual effect on consumer surplus. In essence, this flips the logical relationship: instead of the degree of market competition leading to higher or lower consumer surplus, we have changes in consumer surplus determining to what degree competition exists. In other words, competition is no longer understood independently of antitrust, but in relationship to it. What's more, this shows that competition stands in a distinctly secondary relationship to antitrust and its focus on consumer surplus (and total welfare), which exemplifies the way antitrust treats businesses and their owners simply as a means to the end of benefiting society, rather than as valuable members of society themselves.

The second point follows, and it should be a familiar one by now: none of the exclusionary actions we've discussed violate any recognized rights of consumers or competitors. They are all valid exercises of firms' property rights that should be protected from legal scrutiny, not be subject to it. To be sure, the general category of exclusionary practices includes plainly criminal or tortuous actions, including acts of coercion and deceit on the part of one firm that clearly violate the rights of another. One retailer cannot burn down the store of a competitor, threaten competitors' employees out of coming to work, or give false statements to their customers about other stores' products or service. These are wrongful and (justifiably) illegal tactics that violate well-defined rights and therefore fall squarely in the domain of tort or criminal law, and as such they need not be the concern of antitrust.

Actions such as predatory pricing and restrictive contracts, however, violate no established or recognized rights of competitors (or consumers), regardless of whether their effects on consumer surplus and welfare earn them the label "anticompetitive." Firms have no right against their competitors lowering their prices, even if those prices are low enough to endanger their own livelihood—as noted earlier, this is a normal part of the competitive process, weeding out inefficient firms and increasing consumer surplus. The fact that some firms are larger than others, or have greater ability to withstand losses, should not limit their business options, certainly not in observance of imagined rights on the part of its less able competitors—firms who, in a dynamic market, are likely to be replaced by new competitors eager to prove they can succeed where others failed.

If no rights of competitors or consumers are violated, then the business practices challenged by antitrust authorities under the heading of exclusionary practices are just as legitimate as any other. A business exists to serve its owners' interests, which are usually (and reasonably) assumed to take the form of earning the maximum profit possible within accepted legal and ethical norms.[14] One way, and perhaps the main way, to do this is by way of actions directed toward the consumer, offering goods and services at prices and other terms that satisfy preferences and provide more value than competing firms doing the same. If one firm is more successful than another, the former will gain sales, revenues, and profits, while the other firm loses them (and has no right to them that would protect against these losses). In this sense, the more successful firm "excludes" the less successful firm from some of the profit it could have earned, albeit indirectly through earning the business of consumers.

This mode of competition may seem ideal or "cleaner," especially when using the American football analogy I gave above, but this does not mean that other competitive actions are illegitimate or unfair in any meaningful sense (discussed more below). Let's consider another common example of exclusionary practices: exclusive contracts. When one firm signs a contract securing exclusive rights to a key supplier or access to a prominent retailer, the opportunities of competing firms may be limited, but competitors had no right to those opportunities—to the contrary, they have every right to form those arrangements themselves (and may do with respect to other suppliers or retailers). If these deals foreclose access to a related market altogether—if the supplier or retailer is a monopoly themselves—this only increases the incentive for new firms to enter their market (as collusive price increases do). If there are economic or financial factors preventing this, such as the size of the relevant market, high fixed costs, or prohibitively high costs of entry, this is unfortunate for firms who are left out of the exclusive agreement, but does not grant them any new rights to prevent it.

In some cases, these exclusive contracts may take the form of vertical mergers, in which firms at different levels of the production process join together, such as a manufacturer combining with a supplier of raw materials, or a wholesaler combining with a retailer. In this case, the same restrictions on trade exist, but they come with increased cost efficiencies through the elimination of "double marginalization." For example, a fabric producer selling to a separate clothing manufacturer will charge a price above its production costs to earn an acceptable profit margin, and the manufacturer will do the same thing when setting its price for sale to its customers. The eventual price to consumers reflects both levels of mark-up, or double marginalization. However, if the two firms merge and become divisions of the same company, the resulting firm only needs to mark up its price once, an efficiency that results in lower prices to consumers. This explains why economically-oriented antitrust authorities are much less concerned with vertical mergers than horizontal ones: horizontal mergers are expected to lower consumer surplus and total welfare, while vertical mergers are more likely to increase them.

From the viewpoint of rights, however, they are identical, both representing an exercise of property rights that violates no rights on the part of consumers or competitors. Horizontal mergers may be bad for consumers and good for the merged firm and its competitors, but it lowers consumer surplus and total welfare, so it is scrutinized by antitrust authorities. Vertical mergers may be bad for some competitors and good for the merged firm and consumers, but it has the potential to raise consumer surplus and total welfare, and is therefore not as often scrutinized. This is entirely utilitarian calculation, though—neither type of merger is doing anything wrong in the sense of violating recognized rights of other parties.

In general, the problem with antitrust's concern with exclusionary practices is that it delineates a very specific form of competition that, despite appearances, is concerned more with welfare than fairness. As we saw above, vertical mergers and exclusive contracts both affect commerce in the same way and to the same extent, so they both should be judged to be equally "unfair." However, because vertical mergers have the potential to lower prices and increase consumer surplus and total welfare, they are permitted, whereas exclusive contracts are more often scrutinized (and allowed only if their negative effects on welfare are minimal). If all exclusionary practices were truly considered unfair and wrong, they would not be allowed even when they increase welfare, demonstrating that antitrust advocates' arguments from fairness, like any invocation of rights in traditional economics, ultimately collapse to welfare in the end.[15]

Even if fairness were a sincere concern on the part of antitrust advocates, it remains an arbitrary definition. Take my analogy to sports and other competitions above, in which participants are not allowed to interfere with each other's performance. This seems entirely and intuitively fair, so why shouldn't this sense of fairness extend to business competition as well? To answer this, we need to consider the purpose of each instance of competition. Sports serve many purposes, but a prominent one is entertainment: fans want to see an exciting game or match, and rules are often established in part to serve this purpose. In American football, little is more thrilling than watching a receiver run halfway down the field and catch a ball thrown from 50 yards anyway. This would happen much less often if a player on the opposing team could simply push or tackle a receiver before they had a chance to catch the ball. There is nothing intrinsically fair about prohibiting pass interference—this rule could just as easily be seen as unfairly removing a lucrative option from the playbook of the other team. But it does make for a more exciting and dramatic football game.

What about the competition between managers for a promotion at work? Certainly this would be closer to business competition than a football game, but the design of this type of competition is no less tailored to its specific purpose. We would naturally assume that the firm wants to promote the best person for the job, and the rules of the competition are designed to give them that information. (In a similar way, another purpose of sports is to highlight the best athletes, either individually or as teams, although to some this may be secondary to the entertainment value—and therefore the financial value.) If the firm is interested in evaluating the potential of each managerial candidate, they would want to rule out any behavior that would interfere with this goal, if not speak against it entirely. Not only would underhanded sabotage of one candidate by another defeat the informational purpose of the competition, especially if the victim of the sabotage is in fact the best candidate, but it would likely also represent character traits the firm would not want in their newly promoted employee! Here too, a rule of non-interference is not fair in and of itself, but rather is instrumental to the purpose of the competition itself.

So what are the goals of competition? We shall have more to say about this in the final chapter, but for now we can simply say that they are not necessarily what antitrust authorities and advocates imagine them to be. Rather than being a means to increase welfare or consumer surplus—or generate tax revenue or provide employment, as other government agencies might think—business competition is properly regarded as emerging from the interaction of firms and consumers exchanging money, goods, and services according to their property rights (assuming they do not violate the rights of others). More generally, it represents the use of one's resources to pursue one's interests in the context of market exchange, from which competition may emerge if the conditions are suitable.

Understood this way, business competition does not serve any purpose of its own, and rather is incidental to economic activity. Of course, it has definite beneficial effects to consumers (in the form of low prices) and the economy as a whole (in terms of efficiency and welfare). But, as I have argued through this book, these beneficial properties to some parties do not justify interfering with the free and valid exercise of property rights in market exchange. To do this is to treat business owners as simply means to the ends of consumers and society as whole, which violates the most basic terms of respect owed all persons (to borrow Kant's language). Furthermore, to restrict this exercise of property rights in the name of an arbitrary conception of fairness that was imposed purely to advance this goal, for which business owners are nothing more than a tool, does offense to the very idea of fairness as well as respect.

So far in this book I have focused much more on the rights of the various parties involved in commerce, which I hope is understandable, given the lack of attention paid to rights in economics, including economic discussions of antitrust. Although I have acknowledged the harm done by firms in the process of doing business, both to consumers and competitors, perhaps I have not given that side of the picture sufficient attention. This will be remedied in the next chapter, in which we look at how economists look at harm in the absence of rights, and the problems with this—and we'll start by questioning a central concept in economics that says much about its approach to antitrust as well.

6

Harms and wrongs

One of the ideas I have emphasized throughout this book is the distinction between harm and wrong, which is usually ignored in discussions of economics in general and antitrust in particular. In most of these discussions, the mere existence of harm is sufficient to motivate a policy response—and not just motivate it, but justify it as well. Ironically, even though harm is a central focus of economic decision-making, it is not treated as an absolute wrong that must be eliminated—in fact, there is no concept of a moral wrong in economics or, as we've seen in antitrust, especially as considered by economists.

In this chapter we'll explore this distinction in more depth. We start by examining a common example of its neglect in economics, the critique of which opens the door for important legal concepts, which themselves are controversial elements of the economic approach to law (also known as "law and economics"). Although this chapter does not address antitrust as directly as most, it does enlighten several of the discussions to this point while setting the stage for those to come in the rest of the book.

EXTERNALITIES

Perhaps the most pernicious example in economics of the confusion between harm and wrong is the *externality*. As all students in introductory economics courses are taught, an externality occurs when a transaction between two parties affects someone who has no part in it.

(For this reason, externalities are sometimes called *third-party effects*.) Externalities can be positive or negative: for example, homeowners who take good care of their property make the neighborhood more attractive and increase the value of their neighbor's property, and homeowners who do not take care of their property have the opposite effect.

Although it is a part of the standard definition used in economics, with its focus on the third-party effects of market activity, the existence of a commercial transaction is not essential to the identification of an externality. In general, an externality occurs whenever one person's actions inadvertently affect another person's interests (for better or for worse). The implication is that if the other person had been consulted, or if their interests had been considered, the external effects could have been managed better.

In terms of law and policy, negative externalities are obviously the greater concern, but there are costs to positive externalities too, specifically in terms of unrealized benefit. Continuing with the example above, let's assume the conscientious homeowners who take excellent care of their house do it purely for their own reasons, and they are not thinking about their neighbors when they decide how much time, money, and effort to put into their property. In the language of economics, they are choosing their level of upkeep to maximize their own utility given the costs they face and the benefits they realize (based on their preferences). If they also valued the incidental benefit their property maintenance provides to their neighbors, economic theory predicts that they would increase their level of upkeep to maximize the net benefits to everyone in the neighborhood.

Interestingly, the existence of a positive externality signals that the effect on other parties is actually too small: if the people causing the positive externality took account of the benefits they were providing to others, and treated it as if it were additional benefit to themselves, they would do more of whatever created the positive externality. (Imagine you learn that something you enjoy doing around the house also makes your partner or roommate happy—this would give you incentive to do it even more.) Again, in economic terms we would say the level of the activity creating the positive externality is suboptimal, leaving unrealized benefit on the table, in the same way that a level of market output less than the perfectly competitive level leaves potential consumer surplus and total welfare unrealized (in the form of dead-weight loss).

The typical policy suggestion in this case is to subsidize the behavior creating the positive externality, which gives the responsible party incentive to do more of it, even if they don't care about the benefit enjoyed by others—in other words, if they are the usual self-interested agent of economic models. In essence, the subsidy simulates concern for the well-being of others by making it in the person's own interest to do what is good for others. This is one way to think of government subsidies for environmentally-friendly home improvements such as installing solar panels: the subsidies let homeowners realize for themselves the benefits they can create for others. Without the subsidies, they might not feel that installing solar panels is worth it to them based on their own cost–benefit calculation. But if the government passes on to them some of the benefit this would provide to others—in other words, helping them to *internalize* the externality such action would create—homeowners are more likely to make the decision that is best for everyone.[1]

Whereas positive externalities are an example of a good thing that could be even better, and as such are not often a serious concern for government authorities, negative externalities are a different story altogether, comprising most of the scholarly and policy attention given to externalities in general. Negative externalities result from one or more parties' activity imposing costs or harms on an unrelated third party, such as the negligent homeowners letting their property go to rot and dragging down the property values of their neighbors—or the more commonly discussed and economically significant example of pollution imposed on nearby communities from industrial production.

Although the direction of the effect is different, the underlying theory is the same: negative externalities result from one person not taking into account the effects—in this case, negative effects—of their behavior on others. The firm creating the pollution is making their decisions regarding what, how much, and how to produce based on maximizing profit, or the difference between their own benefits (revenues) and their costs. If they also paid attention to the costs their activity imposed on others and treated them as if they were their own costs, they would make different decisions resulting in less pollution: either less output, different products, or different production technology, whichever would limit the resulting pollution at the lowest cost to the firm. In the absence of such consideration, however, the firm operates inefficiently from society's point of view, producing too much output (or producing it in a more harmful way) because it does not take into account the costs or harms it imposes on others.

One way to get people who create negative externalities to take the costs they impose on others into consideration is through taxation, the inverse of the subsidies used to correct positive externalities. If negligent homeowners were charged a fee whenever their upkeep is judged to be poor enough to affect their neighbor's property values, they would have incentive to increase their efforts. The fee "helps" them to internalize the costs they're imposing on their neighbors, making it in their interest to act in the interests of others. In the same way, fees or taxes applied to polluting firms based on their output, technology, or emissions can lead them to make more environmentally-friendly decisions by making the costs they impose on others part of their own business costs.

If these taxes are calculated precisely enough, the result could be the socially optimal decision in which the costs of production, including the harms caused by pollution, are offset by the benefits of production to total welfare.[2] It is important to note that this does not mean pollution will be eliminated—instead, it will be reduced to the "efficient" level where its costs are justified by the benefits of the output of which it is a byproduct. Eliminating the pollution altogether would mean closing the plant, or at least the specific aspect of production that results in emissions. That would obviously benefit those affected negatively by the pollution, but it would come at significant cost to the business owners and their customers (who would lose a source of a product they valued and would presumably pay a higher price for it elsewhere), not to mention the firm's employees and other parties with a stake in the firm's business. Although the state of affairs in which the firm is allowed to pollute as much as it wants may impose unacceptable harms on those who suffer from the emissions, forbidding production altogether imposes significant harms on other parties.

Assuming there are some methods available to limit pollution without halting production altogether, such as updating technology or making modifications to the product, the most efficient result lies somewhere in the middle: the firm takes steps toward limiting its emissions, reducing its impact on the surrounding community, while remaining in business. In theory, the properly calculated tax or fee can generate this outcome, which maximizes total welfare, including consumer surplus, profit, *and* the well-being of those affected by pollution. In reality, achieving the precise optimal level of pollution would take an incredible amount of information, but even a roughly estimated fee structure that approximates the ideal can potentially achieve significant improvements in welfare.

This is the standard treatment of externalities in economics, and is familiar to readers who have had even a brief introduction to the topic. The reader may have noticed that rights were never mentioned, although they were always in the background of the discussion. For example, the polluting firm's right to operate, even if it creates harmful pollution, is never questioned; nor is the community members' right to have their harms addressed. The only question posed was how to minimize the costs or harm to both parties relative to the benefit of continued production.

The approach of using a tax or subsidy to influence the party causing the externality by changing their incentives—generally called *Pigouvian taxes and subsidies* after Arthur C. Pigou, the economist who introduced both the idea of externalities and how to solve them—is more subtle than simply mandating or ordering the desired change in behavior.[3] Consider outright bans on the use of certain production methods that are judged to be extremely harmful, such that there is no "efficient" level of their use—or homeowners associations (HOAs), who simply require that property be maintained according to certain standards. The subtle manipulation of incentives can definitely be considered to be more respectful of rights, including property rights, than absolute commands limiting or prohibiting behavior.

Although these rights are presupposed in the foregoing analysis, they played no role in the analysis of the problems themselves or their solutions. This is consistent with the general economic approach to rights, which is to take them for granted and then apply utilitarian techniques from welfare economics to address problems. But this neglect of rights significantly limits the way that economics identifies problems, which only appear if someone is harmed, regardless of the source of the harm or its relation to rights, which in some cases take precedence over the harms resulting from their exercise.

EXTERNALITIES AND RIGHTS

Both of the examples used above, private residence upkeep and industrial pollution, involve harm to parties from activities they are not involved with, but are otherwise very different in their scale and importance. There is another difference between them that is less obvious, but is more important to our present discussion and to the arguments over the ethics of antitrust: the existence and nature of the rights involved in each.

Let's begin with the negligent homeowners and their neighbors, which is the simpler case. (It also has much more in common with antitrust than the pollution case does, for reasons that will soon be clear.) Although the lack of upkeep on the part of the negligent homeowners definitely imposes costs on their neighbors in terms of lower property values (as well as a less attractive area in general), we must ask if these homeowners are wronging their neighbors in any way. In other words, familiar from previous discussions, have they violated any recognized rights of their neighbors? Do homeowners have rights or claims to a certain level of aesthetic (and financial) value in other neighbors' homes? Do they have a right to a certain value of their own property, a right that is violated by any actions of others that threaten to lower it?

Unless they reside in a gated community with rules imposed at the time of purchase, or a municipality with very strict maintenance codes, the general understanding of property rights is that homeowners can maintain their property to whatever degree they want, provided it does not prove a danger to the health or well-being of others. For example, a homeowner should not keep rusty sharp tools or cans of spoilt food in their lawn near the sidewalk or the road, or neglect to fix broken windows when glass may fall on neighbors or passersby. Those actions would threaten to violate the legitimate safety rights of others, and would therefore be wrongful. But failing to mow a lawn frequently enough, letting paint peel off the house, or having broken windows that are unattractive but not a safety hazard, do not violate any normally recognized rights of neighbors. As unattractive as these conditions may be, and as much as they may affect neighbors' property values, they would normally be considered fully within the usage rights included in the homeowner's "bundle" of property rights.

If these examples do not convince you, consider if your neighbors took issue with the color you paint your house, the assortment of your holiday decorations, or the message on a flag or sign you display outside in support of a political or social cause—any of which can have the same impact on property values as an unkempt home, depending on the preferences of potential buyers. The general point is that having an unattractive home in one's neighborhood may impose costs on neighbors, which qualifies as a negative externality—but not only does this behavior violate no rights, it is behavior that is protected under the homeowners' property rights. An over-eager economist or policymaker sees a situation like this and imagines how they can change incentives to solve it, but they should consider first whether there is any problem at all.[4]

Can we think of more examples of this type of "problem"? Yes, we certainly can, because they are quite common:

Mike drives to the post office and beats Peter to the parking space right in front of the door, forcing Peter to find a spot farther away.

Susan and John ask for the same high-profile assignment at work, and Susan gets it.

Jane gets into her car and drives to work during rush hour, adding to traffic congestion and extending the commuting time of every other driver on the road.

Alice opens a coffee shop on the same block as Nancy's coffee shop, lowering Nancy's profit through increased competition.

All of these examples, and many more you can easily think of, involve one person being harmed as an incidental result of the choices of others. As Richard Epstein notes, these harms are "*damnum absque iniuria*: economic losses that go uncompensated because they were not preceded by any violation of right."[5] These situations are frequent and ordinary, an inevitable consequence of living in a world with other people, especially when scarcity rears its ugly head. Whether it's grabbing the last cherry danish at the bakery, getting the last available Beyoncé ticket, or placing an obnoxiously complicated order at the coffee shop ahead of a sleepy author under deadline who just wants his large black coffee so he can get back to work, many of our ordinary everyday activities impose real costs on others, albeit small ones in most cases. But do these activities violate any recognized rights of those who are harmed? No. And are the harmful activities within the rights of those performing them? Yes.

What's more, some of these activities are encouraged, such as the competition between Susan and John for the assignment and between Alice's and Nancy's coffee shops, because they have broader purposes: finding the best person for the job and generating consumer surplus and welfare (respectively). As we saw in Chapter 2, business competition can be brutal under the right conditions, resulting in profits that only cover opportunity costs. Every new entrant that joins an existing industry forces the rest to lower prices and lose profits, a clear example of an externality—but one that is accepted and encouraged in the broader goal of increasing total welfare. But even without this consideration, and as we discussed in Chapter 4, firms have no rights to a certain price or level of profits that would protect them from competition, and therefore no rights are violated from new firms entering an industry and competing with existing ones.

The only one of the four examples given above that would arouse the interest of even the most aggressive of policymakers—and it has—is Jane's contribution to traffic congestion during her commute to work each day. This externality is sometimes addressed with *congestion taxes*, such as increased charges during peak times on toll roads, bridges, and tunnels.[6] These charges lead drivers to internalize the costs their presence is imposing on other drivers—which is, to say, each other, because in this case there are no "innocent victims," with all drivers imposing extra costs on each other. Congestion taxes will lessen traffic only if some drivers can commute at other times (or by other routes), which implies that the extra charges hit those commuters with less flexibility with respect to timing in their jobs.

When we try to parse out the role of rights in this example of externalities, which receives significant attention from authorities, we run into even more trouble than before. The idea that some drivers' rights are being violated by the presence of other drivers on the road at the time is odd, given that these other drivers would also be violating the same rights of yet other drivers at the same time. More important, no one has a right to light traffic and a certain length of commute, a right that would be violated by too many other drivers choosing to go to work at the same time. Policymakers may defend this on the grounds that the congestion taxes are lessening traffic for commuters who need to get to work at that time, who should be willing to pay for the privilege, but this is not a choice for many (if not most) drivers. One could say they are being penalized for where they live in relation to their work—which they already were, in terms of commute length, but they must now pay congestion taxes on top of it, in exchange for slightly less time on the road. As with their work schedules, however, this exchange is not voluntary, and more to the point, it does not address any violation of rights. Excessive commute times are a problem, true, but one borne of scarcity, and one that already carries significant costs—which do not need to be worsened in an effort to reduce harms (to the same people paying the tax) who are violating no rights (of each other).

If we look at the traffic congestion situation differently, especially given that no rights are violated, we can see it as an example of a potential *positive* externality rather than a negative one. Drivers with flexible schedules who can choose to commute at off-peak times are providing uncompensated benefit to drivers who must drive at rush hour. Seen this way, the appropriate policy response in the interest of welfare would be to subsidize drivers who can drive at different times, rather than penalize the ones who cannot. The way you look at it depends on what you regard as the status quo: few drivers on the road, who are harmed by additional ones, or many drivers on the road, who are helped by those who drop out. Given that the situation starts with the latter, it seems more natural to look at this as a case of positive externality.[7]

Of course, there are externalities that *do* involve a violation of rights. For instance, any activity that incidentally damages a person or their property would be such an externality. Jane doesn't violate any other driver's rights merely by driving at the same time, but if she causes an accident that damages another driver's car, or injures the driver or passengers, their rights to the safety of their body or property is violated. The negligent homeowners don't violate their neighbors' rights by letting their lawn become overgrown, but they do if they dump trash out the window and some of it lands on a neighbor's lawn (or passersby). Perhaps most prevalent and harmful—but also more complicated—is the polluting factory that violates local residents' rights to bodily safety and health with its poisonous emissions.

These externalities are distinguished in the examples above by their wrongfulness, representing violations of recognized rights as well as impositions of harm. By itself, harm alone is not enough to justify policy action, except in a utilitarian world, because incidental harms are ubiquitous and do not necessarily wrong anyone. (If economists or policymakers want to reduce these harms, they could always try to address the scarcity that leads to them instead of penalizing those who are forced to deal with it.) Actions that violate rights, however, represent an injustice to people that deserves an official response—and even though such a situation counts as an externality, it is the wrongdoing that must be addressed. Unfortunately, economists in general are not well equipped to address wrongdoing (because their models do not formally acknowledge the concept).

TORT LAW AND EXTERNALITIES

Lucky for us, we have lots of people who are very well equipped to do this: lawyers. As you may have noticed, all the wrongful externalities mentioned above sound like lawsuits waiting to happen. *Tort law* (or accident law) exists to serve precisely this purpose, establishing the conditions under which one party can collect damages or compensation from another party that wrongfully harmed them. A successful tort suit depends on not just the fact that harm was done (as demonstrated by the plaintiff) but that a valid and recognized tort right was violated in the process.[8] As philosopher Joel Feinberg put it, "one person *wrongs* another when his indefensible (unjustifiable and inexcusable) conduct violates the other's right."[9] Another philosopher, Ernest Weinrib, wrote that "the harm has to be to an interest that has the status of a right, and the defendant's action has to be wrongful with respect to that right."[10] Both emphasize that harm alone is insufficient to justify a lawsuit, given its ubiquity in ordinary life; instead, the plaintiff must show that the defendant violated some valid, recognized right in order for a tort case to have merit.

Traditionally, tort law is considered a method to further *corrective justice*, a concept that dates back to antiquity, which holds that wrongs accidentally done to persons should be rectified or "corrected" in some way. (Note that this is distinct from *retributivist justice*, which deals with intentional wrongful harms, which are usually considered crimes, leading to punishment rather than compensation.) The necessity of wrongfulness in cases demanding corrective justice was emphasized by Aristotle, who wrote that, in disputes between private parties regarding harm from an accident, the law is concerned with "the distinctive character of the injury, and treats the parties as equal, *if one is in the wrong and the other is being wronged*, and if one inflicted injury and the other has received it."[11]

This wrongfulness can also be put into terms of duty, as legal scholars John Goldberg and Benjamin Zipursky do in their article "Torts as Wrongs": "Tortious wrongdoing always involves an interference with one of a set of individual interests that are significant enough aspects of a person's well-being to warrant the imposition of a duty on others not to interfere with the interest in certain ways, notwithstanding the liberty restriction inherent in such a duty imposition."[12] Duties not to interfere with protected interests implies the existence of rights against interference with those interests, including the rights to safety of person and property that are violated in the examples of wrongful externality mentioned above. These rights are integral to the wrongfulness that is relevant to corrective justice and tort law; without it, there is simply no legal matter to be settled. As legal scholar Mark Geistfeld writes, "what one has lost for purposes of legal analysis depends on what one was legally entitled to in the first instance"—in other words, what one has a legitimate right to.[13]

The need for rights to be violated in a valid tort case is key to thinking about the non-wrongful externalities discussed above, such as beating someone to the last parking space, slowing down fellow commuters at rush hour, or winning a treasured work assignment. As Goldberg and Zipursky write, given the wide range of interests that can be harmed, "courts and legislatures have never sought to render interferences with all such interests actionable," adding in parentheses that "there is no tort for interference with one's ability to obtain a good education or a decently well-paying job."[14] Others agree, such as legal scholars Jules Coleman and Arthur Ripstein, who write that harm alone is not enough for a tort suit, but that the harmful act "must also consist in the invasion of a right," a distinction that "draws a boundary between the misfortunes that are an injurer's bad luck to bear, and those that are to remain the victim's responsibility."[15]

If Jane accidentally damages Stan's car on her way to work, she has generated an externality and violated his rights in the process. In this case, Stan has recourse through the legal system to recover the harms she imposed on him. But if Jane only delays Stan's arrival at his place of work, she still generates an externality, but his rights have not been violated; in this case, he cannot sue to recover lost wages. More important, in *neither* case is there a need for policy action to correct the externality. If rights are violated, the party harmed could sue for damages in court, but if no rights were violated, there is no wrongful act to address.

Ironically, this implies that even when externalities are wrongful and therefore morally relevant, policy action to address them is unnecessary because the legal system is specialized in correcting the wrong and compensating for harm. If there is no wrong done, harm need not be addressed at all, neither by the courts or policymakers; it remains unfortunate but inevitable in a world of sociality and scarcity.

There do remain cases that are not so simple, however, of which pollution is perhaps the most significant example. Although pollution seems to be an obvious case of wrongfully imposed harm, there are many complexities involved that hamper the legal system in addressing it effectively. For example, there are well-known problems with identifying victims and proving cause, usually involving statistical analysis of rates of illness and morbidity in allegedly affected populations compared to others, numbers that defendants' attorneys can argue are attributable to many factors other than their clients' business activities.[16] In this case, policy measures such as taxes and fees on polluters can be justified as a second-best measure to address the harms they create, even though they permit the wrongful behavior to continue and fail to hold the responsible parties to account in court.[17]

This illustrates another paradox introduced when economists and policymakers see wrongful behavior such as pollution simply as activity leading to an inefficient level of harm and not wrongdoing. Seen from this utilitarian perspective, harm can be balanced by benefits, and the only problem is making sure that total benefits net of harm are maximized. This is why economists do not wish to eliminate pollution but merely reduce it to a level where its costs are justified by its benefits, which they call the "optimal amount of pollution."

When students in introductory economics classes first hear this, their heads often tilt to the side like a dog hearing a strange noise. After all, if pollution is a wrong, why are we satisfied with "optimizing it"? Shouldn't we try to eliminate it? Even if this isn't possible, for obvious practical reasons, shouldn't that still be our goal, rather than being satisfied that any wrongfully imposed costs to some are justified by benefits to others? This cognitive dissonance regarding the economic treatment of pollution—as well as crime rates, which economists also seek to "optimize," much to the dismay of those not trained as economists (and even some who are)—is another result of a strictly utilitarian mindset that refuses to acknowledge any meaningful sense of rights and wrongs (only good and bad, better and worse).[18]

ECONOMICS OF TORT LAW

Before returning to antitrust in the next chapter, I should say a word about my description of tort law above. I was careful to say that the *traditional* conception of tort law is related to corrective justice, because that is not the understanding currently in vogue.[19] Much of present-day tort scholarship is influenced by the *law and economics* movement, which applies mainstream economic concepts of efficiency, preference-satisfaction, and welfare-maximization to legal behavior and the design and implementation of laws.[20] The economic analysis of antitrust was a precursor to law and economics in general: although the application of economic theory and logic to the regulation of business practices and market activity was quickly accepted by the economics profession, it took longer for them to embrace the extension of this approach to legal situations outside market circumstances, including crime and punishment.

It did not take long for the economic approach to the law to find a home in legal education and scholarship as well. As legal scholar George Fletcher wrote, "American law professors have been receptive to economic analysis ... because the culture of American law has long had strong ties to utilitarian thought."[21] He goes on to trace out the way this development encouraged the decline in focus on individual rights in favor of total welfare:

> The devotee of [law and economics] writes in a long line of theorists who think that all legal institutions should serve the interests of society. . . . Yet we have traced a remarkable transformation. The discussion begins with Pareto's principles of efficiency, grounded in the values of secure property rights, individual choice, and the necessity of voluntary transactions. In

light of Kaldor's modest amendment ... we end up with a theory
of legal intervention that permits the periodic redefinition of
property rights for the sake of a collective vision of efficiency. A
theory of individual supremacy ends up as a philosophy of group
supremacy. This is a remarkable metamorphosis. Any theory that
can successfully obfuscate the difference between individual
sovereignty in the market and the dominance of group interests
in coercive decision making will surely gain a large number of
followers.[22]

Some of these followers, it surely need not be said, are advocates of antitrust as well.[23]

Not only does law and economics, like economics in general, neglect
rights in favor of welfare, but it also dispenses with any normative concepts related to duty, rights, or justice. With respect to tort law, this
means that the economic approach focuses on the minimization of
costs, including the costs of harm from accidents as well as the costs of
measures to prevent or lessen them, and gives little attention if any to
securing compensation for the harms still suffered by accident victims.[24]
In terms of welfare, saving costs is an obvious good, while compensation is merely a transfer from one party to another, and therefore cancels
out in the total. This should sound familiar from our earlier discussion
of Kaldor–Hicks efficiency, which guarantees that the "winners" from
a policy change can afford to compensate the "losers," but does not
concern itself with actually arranging such compensation because no
rights to it are recognized. (This is entirely consistent with the refusal
to acknowledge any independent property rights in antitrust as well.)

In fact, the most prominent role for rights in law and economics can be found in one of its central ideas, the Coase theorem, but its
limited role there emphasizes how little regard the economic approach
to law has for rights at all. Inspired by Nobel prize-winning economist
Ronald Coase's paper "The Problem of Social Cost"—the most widely
cited paper in all of legal scholarship—the Coase theorem serves as
both a critical response and an alternative to Pigouvian taxes as a
solution for externalities.[25] The Coase theorem states that if property

97

rights are well-defined and negotiation is relatively easy and costless, then the parties to a legal dispute will settle on the lowest-cost solution, regardless of which party holds the controlling property right in the dispute.[26]

The logic is simple—too simple, as the story goes, for the members of the economics department at the University of Chicago to grasp it at first.[27] Coase's main example dealt with railroad trains that threw sparks on farmers' crops as they passed by. Let's say it would cost the railroad $100,000 to install shields to prevent the sparks, and it would cost $200,000 for the farmers to move their crops farther from the tracks. If the farmers' property right in their crops is held to be more important than the railroads right to travel unimpeded, then they can force the railroad to install the shields (at a cost of $100,000). But if the railroad's right is held to be more important, then the farmers would have to move their crops at a cost of $200,000—or the farmers can pay the railroads an amount between $100,000 and $200,000 to install the shields, which would be cheaper for the farmers and the lowest-cost solution overall. This happens only if negotiation is (nearly) costless and property rights are clearly assigned, which demonstrates the importance of both conditions. A common misunderstanding of the Coase theorem claims that these conditions always hold, when Coase was actually trying to point out that this wasn't the case—and that the legal system would run much more smoothly if it was.[28]

In theory, the Coase theorem reduces the courts' role in such cases to determining who has the controlling property right in a given dispute (if it's not clear from the outset), and then letting the parties negotiate (assuming the costs of negotiation are low enough compared to the stakes in the case). One might think that the appropriate assignment of property rights is based on morality: for instance, in Coase's example it would seem that the farmers would clearly have a right to the safety of their crops, which the railroad has no right to damage. To emphasize his point about efficiency, however, Coase treated all harms as reciprocal: "The question is commonly thought of as one in which A inflicts harm on B and what has to be decided is: how should we restrain A? But this is wrong. We are dealing with a problem of a reciprocal nature. To avoid the harm to B would be to inflict harm on A."[29] In the sense that it takes two to tango, it also takes two parties to create an accidental interaction. Although the trains do throw the sparks that damage the crops, there would be no damage were the crops not there in the first place. Despite Coase's focus on efficiency, it is clear that in this case, as in many others, rights are assigned either by common-sense ethics or well-established law, which allows the Coase theorem to work its economic magic providing the parties are able and willing to negotiate over the terms.[30]

If property rights are not clear, however, the court must make a determination, which is where the economic approach to law again shows its disregard for acknowledged rights. According to law and economics, courts should not vest the property right in whichever party has a moral claim to it, but rather in whichever party has the lowest-cost solution to the problem (making any further negotiation unnecessary). In reference to Coase's example of the crops and the trains, Posner asks "what ethical principle compels society to put a crimp in the latter because of the proximity of the former?"[31] This shows that to the economic approach to the law, the existence of pre-existing property rights is not only irrelevant but an unwelcome distraction from the goal of minimizing costs and maximizing welfare.[32]

We are now ready to return to antitrust, which embodies the same conceptual difficulties that we identified with externalities. As we saw in Chapter 5, none of the actions taken by firms that are prohibited by antitrust law violate any recognized rights on the part of consumers or competitors. They often do impose harm in the form of higher prices for consumers or lower profits for competitors, but these are the results of actions taken in expression of basic property rights. In this way, they are similar to the examples of non-wrongful externalities given above, in which one party does something wholly within their rights that does lead to another party experiencing a setback to their interests, but violates no rights.

Nonetheless, such legal prohibitions imply an obligation on the part of business owners to exercise their property rights only in ways that benefit consumer surplus or total welfare. This represents a unique responsibility, not imposed on any other private parties, and not even all business owners—only those with enough influence over market prices and output to significantly affect outcomes. In the next chapter, we'll explore several philosophical and legal implications of this obligation, which reveals new wrinkles in our exploration of the ethics of antitrust.

7

The obligation to maximize welfare

As we discussed in Chapter 6, antitrust enforcement is a case of the government using legal and regulatory means to address a non-wrongful externality. To this end, authorities try to reduce harm that results from anticompetitive behavior even though it violates no rights. However, this type of externality is not addressed by subtly adjusting incentives with Pigouvian taxes or acknowledging property rights to enable the application of the Coase theorem. Instead, the force of law in the form of injunctions or criminal penalties is brought down on firms who conduct their business in ways that fail to maximize welfare.

Looked at another way, the enforcement of antitrust law implies that firms have a responsibility to contribute to, if not maximize, consumer surplus or total welfare. From the perspective of antitrust advocates and enforcers, firms exist not to further the interests of their owners but to benefit society. If they fail to do this to a significant extent, they are breaking the law and can be sanctioned. This may be the most controversial but least appreciated aspect of the nature of antitrust and competition law in general. In this chapter we'll explore several dimensions of this unique obligation, including why it's such a problem, how it can possibly be justified, and what its enforcement implies about the status of prosecuted firms under the law.

TO WHAT LENGTHS?

To be sure, increasing welfare or well-being is a good thing, and not just according to utilitarians. All else the same, nearly everyone believes that making society better off is ethically good, even if it is not necessarily everyone's primary moral focus. But that qualification, "all else the same," is doing a lot of work—the devil, as they say, is in the details.

The literature on utilitarianism is full of "nightmare examples" of people doing horrible things in the interest of maximizing welfare. A common one has a dictator facing a violent popular revolt, so he picks one person out of the crowd and executes them to calm the crowd, saving not only his own neck but also the many lives that would likely have been lost in the uprising. Other examples similarly lean into supervillain territory, such as Ozymandias from the graphic novel *Watchmen*, who fakes an alien invasion to unite the hostile nations of the world against a common enemy. His actions cause tremendous mass death and destruction in New York City, but prevents World War III, which would have likely been much worse.[1] Almost all megalomaniac would-be world saviors sincerely think the world would be better if they ran it; they display a warped sense of altruism that seems reasonable in the realm of fiction, but it becomes chillingly frightening when expressed by a fascist politician in the real world, given the lengths to which they are willing to go to create their vision of a "better world" (for a select few).

On a much smaller scale, the many variations of the infamous *trolley problem* all involve killing one person to save a larger number of others.[2] In the classic version, a runaway trolley carrying five passengers is heading toward a destroyed bridge. A bystander has the opportunity to pull a switch that will divert the trolley to another track, saving the five passengers, but killing a single person who had stumbled onto the other track. Although some may be comfortable killing the one person to save five in this version—a tragic yet reasonable utilitarian calculation—other versions are more fraught. Consider a surgeon who is treating five patients, each of whom needs a different organ transplant to live. Just as the surgeon had all but given up hope that transplant organs would be found, a sixth patient walks in for his annual check-up, as healthy as can be. Should the surgeon kill the healthy patient to save the other five?

The common theme of these philosophical thought experiments is: how far are we willing to go to increase well-being, happiness, or welfare? Again, this is an admirable goal in the abstract, but unless you are a strict utilitarian, there are some moral lines you are probably not willing to cross to further it. As shown in the examples above, this often involves the intentional infliction of harm or injury on persons who in no way deserve it—which can also be understood in terms of the right not to be so harmed. This is another way to frame my argument that the appropriate respect for the property rights of business owners should protect them from the welfare-maximizing policies of the government. As Adi Ayal writes, "at issue is whether an important social function currently being regulated in a certain manner is, or is not, respectful of rights we as a society consider basic, almost sacred," and it's clear that antitrust fails this test.[3]

Of course, antitrust is a far less dramatic example than a murderous dictator, a surgeon considering sacrifice, or a random bystander confronted with a runaway trolley. We are not talking about killing the few in order to save the many, but we *are* talking about a more common-place policy choice that most of us too quickly accept: interfering with individual autonomy in an attempt to generate higher total welfare, or limiting the rightful options of the few to benefit the many.

Antitrust law has more in common with societies in which people are directed or commanded to use their talents and capabilities to benefit the state. In such a world, if a young person shows aptitude relevant to medical practice, they are directed to the necessary coursework towards becoming a doctor or nurse; if they show talent in music, art, or dance, they are sent to the appropriate programs or conservatories. One's vocation is no longer a matter of personal preference or autonomy, but simply what best promotes total welfare as determined by the state. In other words, individuals exist only to benefit the state, not to pursue their own interests. Even if we argue, as John Stuart Mill does, that over-all welfare is most likely maximized by allowing people to make choices in their own interests (which collectively comprise total welfare), this only emphasizes that personal autonomy is valued instrumentally and contingently, not intrinsically and absolutely.[4]

In liberal societies, we don't typically think of individuals as being obligated to make decisions that would benefit total welfare. Those of us fortunate enough to live in such places enjoy the freedom to live where we choose, associate with whom we choose, purchase what we choose, and work as we choose. None of these choices is perfectly free, of course—they all take place within constraints determined by the similar choices of others. But we are allowed to make these choices to further our own interests, whether they be selfish or altruistic, as long as they do not violate the rights of others to do the same. We may choose to make decisions in the interests of society, as do those who take the environmental impact of their actions seriously, but we're not forced to—at the most, we are given incentives to do so by policies such as Pigouvian taxes, but as we pointed out in Chapter 6, this is less coercive than direct orders or commands.

For the most part, business owners are allowed these same freedoms. Most entrepreneurs can start businesses when and where they choose, produce whatever goods and services they choose, offer them for sale at the terms they choose, and manage their personnel as they choose, as long as they respect the valid and recognized rights of their customers and employees. Most firms will never be challenged under the antitrust laws due to the effect of their actions on total welfare—but not because the law acknowledges their rights to engage in activities that do not violate the rights of others. The tacit permission of antitrust authorities is contingent on firms' activities contributing to total welfare—or, if they detract from it, they do not do so significantly enough to justify the officials' attention.

The fact that antitrust exists at all, and that firms are penalized for rightful actions that simply have a negative effect on consumer surplus and total welfare, means that firms have rights only insofar as they exercise them in a way that benefits society. They are allowed to operate as they choose unless that choice is one that, in theory, would likely lead to a substantial decrease in welfare. One firm raising its prices would not have much effect on consumers, especially if the firm faces substantial competition, but several firms colluding to raise prices would—so that is forbidden by antitrust. A merger between two firms out of ten would have little impact on consumer well-being, but a merger between two firms out of three would—so that is forbidden by antitrust. A large firm lowering its prices is great for consumers in the short run, but if that might drive out smaller competitors and lead to higher prices later, that would hurt consumers in the long run—so that too is forbidden by antitrust.

In all of these cases, firms are engaging in behavior that is fully within their property rights as commonly understood and violates no established rights of consumers or competitors. But if this behavior fails to increase welfare, and instead threatens to lower it substantially, it is scrutinized and possibly penalized (or prevented, in the case of a proposed merger).

ECONOMIC AND NON-ECONOMIC RIGHTS

In liberal societies, business owners are unique in receiving this treatment. Consider prominent individuals—who could nonetheless be considered businesses in their own right—whose activities have a significant impact on total welfare. I'm thinking of superstars like Beyoncé, Tom Cruise, or LeBron James, who generate billions of dollars of revenue for themselves and their respective business partners and even more benefit for their fans and supporters.[5] If any of them chose to retire, it would have a significant effect on the economy, but no government agency would interfere or try to prevent this choice. Nor should they: the fact that these individuals are incredibly popular and successful does not diminish their rights to make personal decisions in their own interests. They are free to make decisions that have a significant impact on total welfare, and these choices are rightly considered to be within their personal rights, regardless of the effect on other people's well-being or that of society as a whole.

Again, for most firms, their rights to make business decisions according to their interests usually go unquestioned as well. But the fact that they *can* be questioned, for the sole reason that they are not in the interests of the state, is our main concern. In other words, why are the rights of business owners given less weight or emphasis than the rights of individuals?

We can approach this issue from a slightly different direction and ask why liberal societies value and protect economic rights less than non-economic (or "personal") rights. Individuals are free to make their own choices regarding their personal lives, especially regarding what they say, where they live, or who they love, but choices regarding how money and resources are used, especially in a commercial setting, are more often and thoroughly scrutinized.

This distinction has been defended on utilitarian grounds. For instance, after emphasizing the benefits of commerce in terms of the welfare it generates, John Stuart Mill argued that the state is free to regulate economic activity in the name of welfare because liberty and commerce are unrelated:

> This is the so-called doctrine of Free Trade, which rests on grounds different from, though equally solid with, the principle of individual liberty asserted in this Essay. Restrictions on trade, or on production for purposes of trade, are indeed restraints; and all restraint, *qua* restraint, is an evil: but the restraints in question affect only that part of conduct which society is competent to restrain, and are wrong solely because they do not really produce the results which it is desired to produce by them. As the principle of individual liberty is not involved in the doctrine of Free Trade, so neither is it in most of the questions which arise respecting the limits of that doctrine ... Such questions involve considerations of liberty, only in so far as leaving people to themselves is always better, *cæteris paribus*, than controlling them: but that they may be legitimately controlled for these ends, is in principle undeniable.[6]

As philosopher John Tomasi notes, Mill is not the only thinker who disvalued economic rights: for example, John Rawls "makes no special place for the economic liberties of capitalism," speaking only of limited ownership rights and the right to choose an occupation.[7] He also finds the crucial documents of liberty rights, such as the United States Declaration of Independence and the United Nations Universal Declaration of Human Rights, lacking in this regard.

As Tim Wu writes, Justice Louis Brandeis himself "took the view that government's highest role lay in the protection of human liberty and the provision of securities consistent with human thriving." But this view was bifurcated: "That meant a commitment to civil liberties, like rights of free speech and privacy, protected by the courts. But it also meant a commitment to the protection of workers, and an open economy composed of smaller firms—along with measures to break or limit the power of monopolies."[8] The last commitment, of course, can be pursued or achieved only by the denial of economic rights, especially to owners of monopolies. Elsewhere, Wu paraphrases Brandeis again when he writes that "for most people, a sense of autonomy is more influenced by private forces and economic structure than government."[9] But this language casts individual autonomy in opposition to "private forces," when the latter are expressions of individual autonomy as well. All of our freedoms are necessary and naturally limited by the freedoms of others, but some would further restrain economic freedoms to non-economic ones.

Despite the prevalence of the distinction between "personal" and "economic" rights, it is very difficult to make a principled argument for why some choices are more worthy of protection than others. How a person spends her money or uses her "working" time is no less a personal choice than how she chooses to live or who she chooses to love, just because the former is financial or commercial in nature. In fact, few of the choices we usually consider personal or private are made in the absence of economic considerations, as anyone who has bought a house, planned a wedding, or raised a child knows. Every choice an individual makes is personal, and nearly every one of those choices involves resources to some degree, which makes them economic choices as well. Once this is recognized, as Epstein writes: "Protection of economic interests should extend no further, but no less far, than protection of other personal and private rights. Once a theory is developed that addresses both the scope and limitations of individual rights, its consequences cannot be disregarded simply because they clash with the dominant sentiment as to what counts as good and proper social control."[10] To do otherwise would, as noted earlier, defeat the very purpose of rights as "trumps" against welfare. Accordingly, Epstein stresses that "private property and individual autonomy are the only trumps we have" and "the autonomy they demand in personal matters—marriage, religion, speech—apply with equal force in general economic matters as well."[11]

The implicit argument for treating economic rights differently from non-economic rights may be that, because economic choices have a more substantial effect on welfare, regulation and oversight are required to ensure that this effect is positive (or not very negative). But this position rests as several fallacies. First, just because welfare can be measured (in theory) does not imply that it must be managed and maximized by the government. Just because something *can* be done doesn't imply that it *must* be done, even if it had no impact on individual rights—an affirmative argument must be made for such an exercise of government power, even if that argument would be obvious in the context of utilitarianism.[12]

Second, the statement that economic choices uniquely affect welfare depends on the fact that welfare is most often calculated in economic terms. Naturally, when a large company raises price or shuts down a factory, those actions are going to affect welfare as defined by economists. A world-famous celebrity or politician who makes offensive statements that threaten the safety of a minority group may have a similar effect on well-being understood in more general terms of happiness or mental health—as well as physical health if the speech encourages violence—but the effects of this on economic measures of welfare are likely to be indirect and go unnoticed.

Finally, the mere fact that the effects of economic activity happen to be noticed, measured, and appreciated does not void the rights that protect it. Acts of speech often have significant effects on societal well-being but are nonetheless protected—and rightly so—as are acts in expression of sexual freedom that threaten to upset more delicate sensibilities. But once personal decisions have a significant impact on welfare as understood in economic terms, such protections are often dispensed with and demands are made that such activity not reduce welfare—again, implying a responsibility on the part of economic actors to promote welfare (if not maximize it outright).

The refusal to protect individual property rights when they are exercised in a commercial context also invokes the tyranny of the majority, another of Mill's concepts, which we discussed in Chapter 4. Recall that this term refers to the tendency of a majority in society to suppress the interests and rights of a minority, either through informal social means or formal democratic processes. The tyranny of the majority is used most often to describe efforts of majorities in society to enact legislation, through legitimate democratic processes, to limit the activity of minorities, usually defined in terms of race, gender, or sexual orientation. Individual rights exist to prevent this, "trumping" welfare (in the words of Ronald Dworkin quoted earlier) and thereby protecting the minority from exactly this type of government action motivated by utilitarian concerns. In effect, these rights send a message that, as important as promoting well-being and welfare is, some freedoms are more important.

It would be churlish of me to argue that the right of firms to conspire to raise prices to boost their own profits is on the same moral level with the rights of oppressed persons to enjoy the same basic human freedoms as everybody else. Clearly these are two very different things—not only in the relative depth of their impact on human dignity, but also in the fact that, in the case of antitrust, the minority is a group that is normally regarded as powerful and which imposes actual harm (rather than mere offense) on the majority.[13] Because of this, perhaps, it is easy to overlook the fact that antitrust law imposes obligations on business owners to promote overall well-being that are not imposed on others, obligations that are a result of what is, nonetheless, a tyranny of the majority.

Despite these differences, the two cases share the common element of a majority acting to suppress the rights of a minority—of which some explicitly approve. For example, Wu writes that because of the influence of Robert Bork's restrained approach to antitrust, "with narrow exceptions, mainly related to price-fixing, the government was once again barred from trying to influence economic structure, regardless of what Congress said or did. The belief that really mattered was that the market enjoyed its own sovereignty and was therefore necessarily immune from mere democratic politics."[14] Although he frames it as a criticism, his wording is spot on: ideally, business owners would be free to exercise their property rights, as long as they don't violate the rights of others, no matter what the voters say about it, just like acts of speech, worship, or marriage. As we saw in Chapter 4, essential rights should not be subject to democratic debate—and this includes rights all too often diminished as "merely" economic in nature.

CATASTROPHIC HARM AND THRESHOLD DEONTOLOGY

One can accept this argument but respond that the harm done by anticompetitive behavior is so great that state action is justified in preventing it despite the impact on rights. Think of the pollution, as discussed in Chapter 6: because it is very difficult to identify specific parties who are directly harmed (and whose rights are violated) by emissions, the state is forced to take less precise regulatory measures because the total harm imposed on the overall community is substantial enough.[15] The case of anticompetitive behavior is somewhat different, chiefly because it violates no recognized rights, but there is significant harm, which may justify legal intervention nonetheless. Is there a point at which the harm from anticompetitive behavior becomes large enough that the state is justified in acting to prevent or lessen it, even if the behavior that caused it is not wrongful and the property rights of business owners will be compromised?

The quick answer is yes: there is an ethical argument for this, but like the tyranny of the majority it comes from an unlikely place. Recall from Chapter 3 the school of moral philosophy known as deontology, which judges actions in general as right or wrong instead of assessing specific instances of them as good or bad. A frequent criticism of deontology, especially from utilitarians, is that without any consideration of the costs or consequences of actions that are considered right or just, deontologists end up taking the position of *fiat justitia ruat caelum*, or "let justice be done though the heavens fall." Such a stance can be seen as noble and admirable, especially when someone sticks to their principles no matter the cost—as long as the costs are borne by the person taking the principled stand. But if the cost of one person's moral position are borne by others, it is more difficult for that person to stick by that position. We see this often in action stories in which the hero is forced to back off after the villain threatens a hostage. This puts the hero in the position of what philosophers call a *tragic dilemma*, from which "one cannot escape with clean hands": they either have to let the villain escape or allow the hostage to be harmed, neither of which is an acceptable outcome.[16]

The legal philosopher Michael S. Moore introduced the concept of *threshold deontology* to address situations where maintaining moral principles had significant and widespread costs. In threshold deontology, once these costs rise above a "threshold" level, decision-makers are allowed, if not required, to abandon the relevant deontological principles to minimize their costs. His motivating example was torture: even if a society opposes torture as a matter of principle, is there an amount of potential harm large enough to justify its use? Imagine a doomsday scenario in which terrorists plant a nuclear bomb somewhere in a large city. The authorities have captured several of the terrorists and want them to reveal the location of the bomb. They are reluctant to use torture, but they also realize that the potential cost of maintaining this position in light of the current threat is the loss of many innocent lives.[17]

As you may have realized, this is yet another variation of the trolley problem, except instead of killing one person to save many, someone has to decide whether to torture someone to save many; both involve the violation of a moral principle to prevent significant harm. One way to trigger a change of heart in a reluctant bystander in a trolley problem is to increase the number of people at risk in the trolley. Suppose you refuse to kill one person to save five. How about ten? A hundred? As opposed as you might be to pulling that switch and killing the one person on the other track, there is likely a number of passengers on the trolley large enough to get you to reconsider.

The torture scenario introduces not only additional magnitude to the situation—millions of lives could be lost in a nuclear explosion in a large city, as we know all too well from history—but also new practical complications stemming from the unlikelihood of eliciting reliable information using torture.[18] So the decision-maker considering torture has to consider violating an important moral principle to engage in behavior with slim chances of saving lives (assuming there is a valid threat to them). However, if there are enough lives at stake, the potential costs of inaction may be large enough to overwhelm any doubts about efficacy or deontological ethics, and the decision-maker may eventually decide torture is justified.

Again, antitrust is not torture—and again it would be churlish of me to draw any direct line between them—but, as with our comparison to the trolley problem, they do share a common property in the abstract. One can accept my argument that antitrust is unjustified in principle because it penalizes behavior in expression of valid rights that violates no other rights, but nonetheless argue that the costs of unrestrained anticompetitive behavior would be so large to justify it regardless. After all, Lee Loevinger, head of the U.S. Department of Justice's antitrust division under President John F. Kennedy, wrote in 1958 that "the problems with which antitrust are concerned . . . are second only to the questions of survival in the face of threats of nuclear weapons in importance for our generation."[19] Hyperbole aside, I imagine many antitrust supporters would embrace the second part of this argument, given their unanimous statements about the catastrophic consequences of lax enforcement (although I would not expect them to acknowledge the violation of business owners' rights that must be suppressed to prevent this harm).

If we accept the logic of threshold deontology, we are left with the question of whether the potential harm from anticompetitive behavior is significant enough—indeed, catastrophic—to overwhelm any principled qualms about antitrust enforcement? Outside of controlled real-world experiments, which are all too rare in economics, there is no way to be sure.[20] In the short term, consumers are harmed by increases in prices and limited availability of goods and services, which may force them to seek out lower-value alternatives or, in the worse-case scenario, go without. Smaller firms who are subject to restraints of trade by larger ones may be similarly forced to invest their resources elsewhere, in terms of location or product mix, perhaps outside of business altogether.

These harms may be significant, but they are also fairly routine. As we noted above, firms regularly raise their prices, change product offerings, or move locations, all with negative effects on consumers. Smaller, less efficient firms find it difficult to compete with larger, more efficient ones even in the absence of any direct anticompetitive activity. Collusion, merger, or restraints of trade may make these harms larger, but is this increase in magnitude significant enough to render them catastrophic in the sense necessary to overwhelm the principled objections to antitrust? Furthermore, these are short-term effects, likely to be lessened in long term by the effects of normal competition: any behavior that results in higher prices and profits will invite new firms into the market, increasing competition and ameliorating the harmful effects.[21]

When we add to this the constant evolution of markets, especially in the high-tech fields that antitrust authorities seem particularly concerned about recently, it suggests that the harm to consumers and competitors from behavior forbidden by antitrust law is not likely to be catastrophic in scale—and even if it were, the situation is likely to be transitory. Unless a firm can grow large enough to transform the very market they're in and secure long-term advantage—as firms such as Microsoft have been accused of—there is little cause to believe the harms of anticompetitive behavior exceed the high level of costs that would invoke any reasonable version of threshold deontology.[22]

Some commentators point to other, more general harms from anticompetitive behavior, such as those who emphasize the effects of such firm action, and the resulting market power and "bigness," on the state of democracy itself. In 1979 Robert Pitofsky expressed "a fear that excessive concentration of economic power will breed antidemocratic political pressures," which Tim Wu cites in his book, adding that antitrust enforcement "should be animated by a concern that too much concentrated economic power will translate into too much political power, and thereby threaten the Constitutional structure."[23] In several recent papers, law professor Daniel Crane has argued that business concentration can contribute to the growth of fascism—and may have, in the Weimar period in Germany—which would clearly provide an example of catastrophic harm that could reasonably justify overriding private property rights.[24]

The basic idea is that larger firms have more influence on politics based on using their substantial financial resources to both support "friendly" political candidates and lobby existing leaders to make decisions in their favor. Ironically, these concerns stand in the way of democracy more than they support it.[25] The first would deny business owners yet another right: the right to support candidates of their choice, consistent with campaign finance laws in general. Larger, more successful firms may have more resources to donate to political causes, but this does not imply they should have fewer rights to do so (in the same way that their size and influence in the market should not limit their property rights).

The second concern is similar: any individual or group in a democracy has the right to appeal to their elected leaders in support of policies they favor. Of course, the implicit suggestion at the heart of this concern is that this lobbying, especially on a grand scale, represents illicit influence if not outright bribery—which would be morally and legally wrong regardless of the source. Legitimate lobbying efforts, however, are an important way for citizens and voters to express their interests to their elected leaders, and if a politician invites influence in excess of this, it would seem to be a criticism more of the politician than of the person or group whose influence they are inviting. To place all the blame for corrupt politicians on those influencing them would be to let the politicians off the hook—which is a result of emphasizing the antidemocratic effect of legitimate anticompetitive business activity and the "bigness" that may result from it. It would seem that cracking down on corruption among politicians is a more appropriate and precise solution than restricting the valid rights of business owners to communicate with them (short of actual bribery).

ANTITRUST VIOLATIONS AS CRIMES

Let's return to the theme of this chapter, which is that fact that antitrust penalizes firms for failing to increase welfare. This is a legitimate goal of governments who are charged with overall well-being, which can take many forms, from total production or income as economic proxies, to more direct (albeit more controversial) measures of total happiness.[26] But it is not a burden that individual actors in a society should have to bear, whether they be individual consumers, workers, or entrepreneurs, or members of cooperatives such as firms, labor unions, or community groups.

Nonetheless, firms are forced to carry this responsibility, at least in the negative sense that they will be punished if they engage in activities that are seen as particularly damaging to consumer surplus or total welfare. Furthermore, the fact that we say that firms are "charged" and "prosecuted" and later "penalized" and "punished" by the government for violations of antitrust law implies that these activities are regarded as not simply harmful but wrong. Specifically, they are wrong in the sense that invokes the power of the criminal law, which justifies a brief excursion into the nature of crime itself and how the law deals with it.

The precise distinction between civil law and criminal law is subject to endless debate by legal philosophers, but several broad lines can be drawn that serve our purposes.[27] Civil law, which includes the categories of tort, contract, and property, deals with disputes between private parties. When you sue your neighbor for damaging your lawn, take your contractor to court for not finishing work on your house in the agreed-upon time, or challenge the ownership of a piece of land, you are engaging in civil law. (If you have done all of the above, you may also be a very litigious person.) The government may be involved in a civil suit, but as a private party, such as when it takes a supplier to court over a contract dispute. Ordinarily, though, the government is not a party in civil suits, and gets involved only insofar as it provides the forum for the case to be heard: a courtroom, a judge, and a jury if necessary. It is up to the injured party to initiate a lawsuit to seek redress from the party that injured them.

Issues in civil cases are understood to be "private wrongs," harms imposed by one party on another in violation of the latter's recognized rights. We saw this earlier when we discussed tort law in the context of externalities: Paul cannot sue Susan for winning the promotion he wanted, but he can sue her for hitting his car in the parking lot after she drank a little too much in celebration. By the same token, contract law and property law establish rights vested in the parties involved, violations of which can lead to lawsuits. Although these violations of rights represent wrongdoing (which is necessary for a valid legal claim), it is a matter of wrongdoing between the two parties in the case, and is resolved in most cases by monetary compensation (or "damages") paid by the defendant. Ideally, this compensation should make the plaintiff or victim "whole," so that they are indifferent in theory between the wrong occurring or not. (This is obviously more likely in cases of property damage than physical injury: one can pay to repair damages to a car, boat, or house, but paying medical bills does not guarantee a complete recovery.)

Criminal law is different in several important ways. In a criminal case, the government is directly involved as the plaintiff (or prosecutor) who initiates a case against someone accused of committing a crime. Out of recognition of the power of the state and the presumption of innocence on the part of criminal defendants, the government must prove its case "beyond a reasonable doubt," as opposed to a civil plaintiff, who must simply convince the court that it is more likely than not, according to a "preponderance of the evidence," that the defendant is responsible for the plaintiff's injuries.

For current purposes, it is the nature of crime itself and society's response to it that are the two most important differences between civil and criminal law. To make things simpler, let's focus on the difference between torts and crimes, which both involve wrongful harms. What, then, justifies the state taking an active role in the one but not the other?

The best answer is that crimes have a broader impact outside the parties who are directly injured, which makes them an issue for the state to address, instead of leaving it to the victims (who are free to pursue a civil suit on their own). The clearest example is murder: other than the victim themselves, their family and friends are the most directly affected parties, but the crime does not only affect them. It also has a wider impact on the community as a whole, who must live with the knowledge that one of their neighbors was murdered. It could have been them instead, or someone they love—and if one person was murdered recently, what's to say another couldn't be murdered soon? The same goes for assault, theft, and many other wrongful harms defined as crimes, all of which have the effect of making us feel less safe, which justifies state involvement in their investigation, apprehension, and prosecution.

This explanation is not perfect, which should not surprise us, given the haphazard way in which the law has developed over the years.[28] There are anomalies: witnessing a horrible car accident can make a person nervous to drive in the area, but it's not a crime, whereas defamation has been treated as a crime, even though it has little effect on anyone other than the victim. These exceptions aside, crimes can generally be understood as wrongful harms that have enough impact on society to justify the involvement of the state in dealing with them.

The more important distinction between crimes and torts stems from the role of the government in their legal resolution: the consequences of a judgment against the defendant. A finding of responsibility in a civil trial leads to monetary damages to compensate the victim, but a guilty verdict in a criminal trial results in punishment. This is an important enough distinction to make the very imposition of punishment sufficient to identify an action as a crime: as legal scholar George Fletcher wrote, "the infliction of 'punishment' is sufficient to render a legal process criminal in nature."[29]

Outside those sympathetic to the economic approach to crime or utilitarianism in general, to whom punishment simply deters future crime by raising its costs to the potential criminal, punishment is understood to have a significant moral weight.[30] This normative value of punishment can be traced to *retributivist* motivations, which regard punishment as being "owed" to the wrongdoer as a matter of justice, or *communicative* reasons, in which punishment is meant to send an important message to the community, including victims, perpetrators, and potential perpetrators, that society will not condone such behavior.[31] Imposing punishment for crimes involves a certain degree of moral condemnation of criminal acts that does not exist in civil cases, in which compensation is the sole focus (despite the necessary aspect of wrongful action).[32]

Although it is not often put into these exact terms, antitrust violations are crimes. While private parties can sue firms in civil court on

117

the basis of antitrust law—which alone grants them the rights which are considered to be violated—the most significant antitrust cases in terms of precedent and publicity are instigated by the government, not in their own interests as a private party, but on behalf of society, which is harmed by the forbidden behavior through the reduction of consumer surplus and total welfare. Furthermore, convictions in antitrust suits carry penalties: fines for companies (or injunctions to prevent the anticompetitive behavior) and fines or imprisonment for individuals.

Due to their nature as crimes, antitrust violations bear the impression of wrongful harms having a broad societal impact that justify the attention of the state. Because "antitrust is often associated with criminality," Ayal argues in a passage quoted in Chapter 4, "those violating it are not seen merely as harming economic efficiency, but violating moral principles and stealing something that does not belong to them."[33] There is no doubt that anticompetitive behavior can impose significant harm, potentially on a large scale (especially if the firms in question operate on a national level). But this doesn't change the fact that, as we detailed in Chapter 6, no rights are violated by collusion, merger, or exclusionary practices, which are examples of non-wrongful externalities. The parties affected by these actions have no rights on which to base a private injury claim—outside of the rights granted them by antitrust law itself—and certainly none that the state must protect using the force of the criminal law. As Epstein writes, when "the state decides to treat monopolies as felons, it acts in a manner that completely undermines the normative distinction between proper and improper—lawful and unlawful—behavior.... No matter what the political rhetoric, street crime or ordinary theft and not cut from the same cloth as antitrust offenses."[34] Put another way, the state has no business criminalizing activity which is not wrongful, much less activity which should be protected as an expression of valid rights, even if it causes incidental harm.

Another useful (if imperfect) distinction between crime and tort is that crime focuses on intentional acts while tort focuses on accidents. If Bob accidentally hits Jill's car from behind on the road, Jill can sue him for damages, but if he slams into her in an act of rage, the state will prosecute him for a crime. As I said, this is an imperfect distinction:

118

for instance, the criminal law does recognize that one can be so reckless or negligent to render the resulting accident a criminal act, such as some instances of involuntary manslaughter. After all, society expects its members to be very careful when there is a possibility of causing a death—such as when driving when pedestrians are present—and even an accidental death can have widespread effects on the surrounding community, even if only due to the perception of dangerous walking conditions. Nonetheless, crime typically involves an element of intent—*mens rea*, or a "guilty mind"—that implies the accused not only harmed the victim and violated their rights, but *meant* to do so as well.[35]

Is intentionality a normal characteristic of antitrust violations? To take the most obvious example, do firms intend to hurt consumers when they collude to raise prices? They may certainly be aware that consumers will be harmed by this, as they would be when any firm raises its prices unilaterally. A collusive price increase will have more impact and create more harm, but does the cooperation of several firms in order to raise prices more effectively imply that they intended to harm consumers? Altering the terms of an offer, even in cooperation with others, is very different from engaging in fraud or selling faulty goods. Firms may want to hurt their competitors in order to lessen competition, but not their customers, on whom they rely for their daily bread. Do they want to get more revenue out of them through higher prices (knowing full well that sales will fall as well)? Yes they do, just as consumers want to get more consumer surplus by taking advantages of discounts and sales. The bottom line is that, like all market effects, the harm experienced by consumers when prices rise is incidental to the workings of commerce. It's not purely accidental, and it may be fully anticipated, but it was not the intent of the firms to harm consumers (nor does it violate their rights), providing yet another reason that treating such activity as a crime is inappropriate.

Furthermore, if antitrust were truly a crime, representing a socially important wrong, ideally it would be prosecuted regardless of the degree of harm caused. Granted, every society has limited resources and cannot pursue every crime committed, so it must prioritize and dedicate scarce prosecutorial resources to the crimes with the most impact. For this reason, murder is given more attention than theft, which is given more attention than jaywalking. (You might be thinking about the attention given to traffic violations, but even though each one has trivial impact on overall welfare, in total they are much more significant.)

To some extent, then, it is understandable and unavoidable that antitrust authorities would devote more time and resources to violations that pose the greatest threat to consumer surplus and total welfare. But when a merger between two firms out of twenty is not subject to review but a merger of two firms out of three is, that can imply one of two things: either one merger is a potential crime and the other isn't, even though they are identical actions merely taken in different circumstances, or they are both potential crimes, but only one is deemed worthy of official attention for practical reasons. The first possibility holds the owners responsible for characteristics of the industry in which they operate, while the second renders *any* merger questionable. The second is certainly more consistent in terms of principle, but represents a more thorough denial of basic property rights. It also implies that less harmful instances of the same crime are not worth investigating, such as lower-value thefts or murders of less "important" persons, which is problematic given the nature of crime as a societal wrong. (This is yet another result of the conflation of wrong, which is absolute, and harm, which is relative.)

This discretion given to antitrust authorities to decide which cases are worth pursuing can also lead to outcomes that sincere advocates of antitrust would disapprove of. In principle, this is no different from any prosecutorial discretion, which can be abused for political or personal reasons, and does not serve as an indictment of antitrust in particular. Given the arbitrary and unrealistic standards of antitrust, however, its enforcers are given much wider latitude to pick and choose cases than most criminal prosecutors. The unattainable ideal of perfect competition and maximal welfare implies an expansive definition of "market power" and "market failure" that can apply to almost any firm in any industry at any time. (We'll discusses both terms more in Chapter 8.) Coupled with the ambiguous nature of the evidence regarding anticompetitive behavior noted in Chapter 2, an overzealous antitrust enforcer can find a *prima facie* rationale to investigate any firm or industry, which even if it goes nowhere can still be very disruptive to business activity.

Furthermore, this discretion can obviously be used for political purposes as well, and administrators in the U.S. Department of Justice and the Federal Trade Commission during both Democratic and Republican administrations have been accused of politically motivated investigations. This point is not integral to the general argument about antitrust in this book, which applies to the vast majority of antitrust cases that are brought out of sincere concern for consumer surplus or total welfare, with no obvious political or partisan bias. Nonetheless, the flimsy philosophical basis for antitrust law does contribute to its potential for abuse, which provides a secondary argument for rethinking its validity in a liberal society.

RESPONSIBILITY OF BUSINESS

We'll wrap up this long chapter on the obligations of business to contribute to consumer surplus and total welfare by asking: is there any reason to believe that business owners in fact have such a special responsibility?

There are several possible arguments in favor of this that deserve to be considered. One is based on the existence of laws that grant some categories of firms special privileges not available in the free market itself, which may justify special burdens on them that are not expected from other members of society. The most obvious example would be laws that grant firms the right to issue shares that limit the liability of investors to their purchase price, therefore absolving them of any share of the excess liability for losses or lawsuits. If you invest $1,000 in a corporation that incurs losses in excess of its total market value, you will lose your $1,000 investment, but you can't be held liable for any other debts and liabilities the firm might have incurred. Although this doesn't allow corporations themselves to avoid all financial liability, it does give them a significant advantage in raising funding because investors do not bear all the risk of managerial decisions.[36]

According to Daniel Crane, "the kinds of concentrations of economic power with which the antitrust laws are concerned usually arise by virtue of the privileges granted by the state through the corporate charter."[37] Even to a skeptic, Crane agrees, antitrust need not represent an illegitimate exercise of state power in violation of property and contract rights if the market power addressed by antitrust arose itself "by virtue of government intervention in the market."[38] As a result, antitrust "plays an important role in checking the occasional monopolistic tendencies that arise when the state creates an artificial person—a corporation—and endows it with super-human powers of aggregation, limited liability, and immortality."[39] If the growth of the modern corporation is understood to have been enabled by the state, this could imply an obligation to use the success generated by those rights to benefit society, perhaps in the form of increasing consumer surplus or total welfare, rather than just maximizing returns to stockholders. As business professor Luigi Zingales writes, when corporations receive limited liability, they "are granted by the State an extraordinary privilege and, thus, the State itself can demand something in exchange for this privilege."[40]

This is a reasonable argument but ultimately a flawed one. For instance, absent evidence that such a "deal" was made explicit, the state has no right to hold business owners up to terms they impose afterwards. The original legislation may be interpreted as a gift, and a very generous one, but recipients of gifts are not obligated to reciprocate, especially along the lines arbitrarily laid out by the gift-giver after the fact. Also, while acknowledging their negative effects on the environment and other factors outside of the purview of antitrust, corporations on the whole have generated an enormous amount of wealth for society, not only for shareholders but also consumers, workers, and governments. In this sense, the laws that created corporations were not simply a gift to them but can be considered a welfare-maximizing engine for society in general, so any criticism that business owners are uniquely obligated to do even *more* could be interpreted as excessively demanding and arbitrary. Finally, if the true problem is the "super-human powers" granted to corporations by the state, then this should be addressed directly through reforming the relevant laws, not "a species of corporate limitation on creatures the state creates" that constrains the exercise of said powers after the fact (however consistent this is with exploiting their welfare-generating potential).[41]

A second argument comes from the philosophical foundations of property law itself. Although it is outside the mainstream understanding of property rights that I have assumed throughout this book, the "bundle of rights" conception of property, in which the state grants particular rights to particular people under particular conditions, can easily accommodate property rights for business owners that carry responsibilities to promote social welfare. For example, philosophers Liam Murphy and Thomas Nagel make this type of argument in defense of taxes: "Private property is a legal convention, defined in part by the tax system; therefore, the tax system cannot be evaluated by looking at its impact on private property, *conceived as something that has independent existence and validity*."[42] This purely instrumental view of property rights, which denies them any prior moral basis, would grant the state unlimited freedom to limit their exercise in whatever way, and for whatever reason, that it sees fit—including prohibitions on the specific uses of property that lower consumer surplus or total welfare.

This conception makes the state the source of all property rights, rendering any such rights enjoyed by individuals contingent on using them in ways that please the state—an idea perfectly consistent with the economic approach to law, but one that is inconsistent with most of the founding ideas of a liberal democracy that grant individuals a significant number of rights not subject to state discretion. For that matter, *all* legal rights are created by the state as a matter of law, including our most basic civil and human rights, but these are often regarded as being grounded in more basic ethical concepts—and defended vigorously on this basis. As I argued above, property rights are no different, but because of the widespread perception that property rights are not intrinsically valuable and can therefore be treated as instrumental to other rights, scholars are more willing to sacrifice them on the altar of public policy.

*

With this chapter behind us, we have almost finished our journey through the economics, philosophy, and legal aspects of antitrust. In the concluding chapter, we'll step back from the fine details to try to get the bigger picture of where antitrust sits in a broader conception of the market, economy, and society, and what the appropriate sense of "competition" is that should motivate our understanding of how these interrelated concepts work.

8

Re-envisioning the market

In the previous chapter (and throughout this book), I argued that, by penalizing anticompetitive behavior, antitrust law holds business owners legally responsible for promoting consumer surplus or total welfare. This runs counter to the appropriate conception of free trade in a liberal society, in which commercial transactions should be treated no differently from any other type of human activity—which is to say they should be permitted as long as they do not infringe the rights of others to do the same. The behavior considered to be anticompetitive under antitrust law falls squarely within the business owners' property rights understood in a moderate, mainstream way, and does not violate any rights of other parties (including consumers and competitors). Nonetheless, such behavior is prohibited, indeed criminalized, because it does not sufficiently contribute to consumer surplus or total welfare.

In this final chapter, we pull back from the fine details to get a general and abstract view of the market, competition, and the government, as it is ideally considered in a liberal democracy that takes the rights of all seriously. As we shall soon see, this view is antithetical to the utilitarian worldview reflected in the economics-oriented and Neo-Brandeisian approaches to antitrust, and in that sense this chapter brings us back to where we began on the first page of this book.

THE NATURE OF THE MARKET AND THE ROLE OF GOVERNMENT

The critique of antitrust law I've presented reflects a particular understanding of the purpose of the market and the role of the government in it, which is very different from how economists and antitrust advocates understand them. So we need to ask the question: what *is* the purpose of the market? (By "the market," I mean the institutions of commerce, including firms, consumers, and the context in which they trade, whether a physical marketplace or online websites.)

There are two general answers to this question, which reflect different perspectives on how the economy, government, and society interact. The first answer is that the market serves society through generating wealth and well-being: supplying goods and services, employing labor, and creating returns on investment. In other words, the market is an instrument to benefit the members of society, and as such it can and should be regulated to ensure that it creates the most benefit possible.

This instrumental understanding of the market is consistent with the utilitarian style of thinking that supports the mainstream economic conception of antitrust law (as well as, in a less precise way, the traditional and Neo-Brandeisian views of it). If the success of the private system of commerce is judged solely on the results it generates, and those results are found to be wanting, the government is justified in intervening in the market (assuming it believes it can improve those results). Because more competition leads to greater consumer surplus and total welfare, the government should promote those market activities that lead to greater competition and discourage and prohibit those activities that lead to less.

However, true to its foundations in utilitarianism, this way of thinking about the market implies that all of its participants are treated merely as means to the ends of society, without giving due consideration to their own interests (or rights). Commercial interaction between business owners, consumers, and workers are considered valuable only insofar as they benefit society as a whole—and if this benefit is seen as insufficient, their interactions can be "managed" in society's interests.

If this sounds extreme, consider the way that the consequences of economic behavior are reported in the media. We often hear that certain behaviors of the part of consumers, workers, or employers, "costs the economy" some billions of dollars per year. Whether the topic is social media use, diet and exercise, or another activity not directly contributing to the economy, the emphasis is on the impact on overall productivity or national output (GDP), not the individuals performing them or directly affected by them. According to a 2016 study by the RAND Corporation on the economic effects of poor sleep:

> on an annual basis, the U.S. loses an equivalent of about 1.23 million working days due to insufficient sleep. This corresponds to about 9.9 million working hours. This is followed by Japan, which loses on average 0.6 million working days, or 4.8 million working hours, per year. With 0.2 million days the UK and Germany have a similar amount of working time lost, corresponding each to more than 1.65 million working hours.[1]

Also, a 2022 Gallup report regarding "quiet quitting" reports that "employees who are not engaged or who are actively disengaged cost the world $7.8 trillion in lost productivity."[2] For countless more examples, simply type "costs the economy" into the internet search engine of your choice. This rhetoric sends the clear message that individuals' activity, especially in the marketplace, is valuable only insofar as it helps to maximize productivity or total output.[3]

But this is not the only way to look at the market, which leads to the second answer to our question about its purpose. This answer focuses on the rights of those participating in commerce rather than the results of that participation for social welfare. According to this view, which we can call *rights-oriented*, the market is a coordinating mechanism that allows individuals to pursue their interests in interaction with others, in a context that respects the rights and maximizes the freedom of all, limited only by the rights and freedoms of each other. According to this view, the success of the market is judged not by the results it generates in terms of total welfare, but by to what degree it allows individuals to pursue their interests consistent with others doing the same.

In other words, the purpose of the market system is formal or procedural, providing a forum for individuals to work with others to promote their goals, whatever they may be, rather than to promote a particular goal of society as a whole. Accordingly, any regulation of market activity

127

should resemble the roles of officials or referees in sports: they make sure the players follow the rules, but they do not have a stake in the outcome, remaining indifferent to which side wins or what the final score is. In the same way, the government has an important role to play in commerce in terms of enforcing property rights and responding to violations thereof, as well as addressing other legitimately wrongful offenses, but not to promote its own vision of what the economy should be.

Let's look at several participants in the market to see how this works. We'll start with a consumer named Mike. Of course, Mike may play other roles in the market—he may be a worker, an investor, a business owner, or all of the above—but for now we'll just consider his activity as a consumer. After contributing to savings, sharing with his family, or donating to charity, Mike spends his after-tax income on various goods and services he wants or needs, based on his interests. To an outside observer, some of his purchases may be frivolous or wasteful, but we can assume that Mike finds these purchases worthwhile.[4]

Although he has the right to use his available income however he chooses (outside of illegal activity), Mike is limited in his choices by the choices of others. For example, he cannot buy a product that no one is offering for sale, such as his favorite variety of coffee, which was discontinued by the manufacturer. He is free to grow it or roast it himself if he wants it badly enough, but it might be prohibitively expensive to make enough just for him (even considering how much of it he would drink). Also, he cannot buy something he can't afford, such as a luxury car or fancy mansion that is out of his price range. And he cannot buy something from someone who doesn't want to sell it, such as an item of signed sports memorabilia that his neighbor owns but refuses to part with. Mike's freedom to spend his money is limited by the equally valid freedoms of others to offer goods and services on the terms they choose (including not offering them for sale at all).

Now let's consider a business owner: Susan, who owns and operates a coffee shop. Susan has chosen to use her financial resources, plus her time and effort, to open a business. She offers a wide range of drinks, assorted pastries, and sandwiches, plus an inviting environment for her patrons to enjoy them while reading, writing, or socializing. Susan does all of this to serve her interests, of which a significant one is to earn a profit, whatever her eventual goals for it may be: to finance her daughter's college, help with her father's medical bills, or simply make a decent living (or an indecent one, whatever that might mean).

Susan has the right to offer her products for sale according to terms she chooses—provided she follows applicable laws regarding health and safety—but, like Mike, her ability to do this is limited by the choices of others. As any business owner does, she has to provide goods and service that consumers in her market want to buy at terms they find acceptable. Specifically, she has to offer an assortment of coffee and food that local consumers enjoy, and at a price they're willing to pay, and if she wants customers to stay in her store she has to offer amenities that they find attractive, such as comfortable chairs, pleasant music, and outlets or sockets (*lots* of them). If she provides a mix of these factors that generates enough business, she'll be able to remain open and earn a profit, but if she doesn't satisfy her customers well enough, she'll either have to modify her offerings, move to a different location, or shut down entirely.

If Susan happens to make the type of coffee that Mike likes, they can do business together. This benefits them both, in the way that any voluntary transaction serves the interests of both parties: Mike gets his coffee, which is worth more to him than the money he pays for it, and Susan gets the purchase price, which more than covers the cost of making Mike's coffee. By facilitating this exchange, the market system has allowed both Mike and Susan to further their interests better than they could have done on their own. And if Susan stops offering Mike's preferred blend, or if Mike's tastes change, he might go elsewhere, which means that both Mike's and Susan's interests are set back a little bit, but this is because they simply don't match up anymore. After all, Mike can't force Susan to serve him the exact coffee he wants, and Susan can't force Mike to keep buying the coffee she offers. Both are free to engage in commerce as they choose, but they have to accept the equally free choices of others in the market.

Even though Susan's coffee shop is very different from the large corporations she buys her beans, food, or supplies from, the same ideas apply to them. Let's say Susan gets her coffee from JavaCorp, a large corporation that provides beans across the country. JavaCorp has massive financial and human resources compared to Susan's store, and a more complicated governance structure, with a board of directors that guides management to act in the interests of stockholders, which is ordinarily assumed to be profit.[5] JavaCorp is free to use its resources in whatever way it chooses—consistent with various laws and regulations governing finances, labor relations, and environmental impact—but it is limited by the actions of its business partners, including Susan (and, by extension, Mike). As long as Susan likes the beans JavaCorp sells at the terms it sets—which is to say as long as her customers continue to pay the price she asks for the coffee she makes from them—she'll buy them. But if she decides to switch suppliers offering better beans or terms, or if JavaCorp changes its beans or terms in a way that Susan doesn't find useful to her interests, then they'll stop working together.

These examples show that the purpose of the market system is to enable individuals to exchange their resources (money, goods, or services) with others in a way that maximizes their freedom to pursue their interests consistent with others doing the same. If two parties realize mutual gains from trade, they'll exchange in that trade; if they don't, they'll each find others to trade with. No one can force others to engage in trade with them, and they may have to change what they're offering to attract trading partners. The market system, as portrayed by the supply-and-demand diagrams that every student in introductory economics classes knows so well, coordinates these activities in a way that enables all parties to pursue their interests in a mutual respectful way.

Of course, this exchange also generates benefit for the trading partners, which contributes to consumer surplus, total profit, and total welfare. In the rights-oriented view of the market, that is merely a positive side-effect: its main purpose is to enable individuals to pursue their interests in exchange with others. The utilitarian, outcomes-oriented view of the market, however, sees the final outcome as the only important aspect, and considers the free promotion of individuals' interests as simply a means to generating it. Furthermore, if the free commercial interaction of individuals does not generate as much outcome as possible, then under the utilitarian view the government should interfere in those interactions so that the outcome can be improved, regardless of the impact on the rights of market participants. If the results are all that matter, anything that can be done to improve them can and should be done.

The rights-oriented view of the market system, which supports the freedoms and interests of market participants, provides a deeper understanding of the critique of antitrust I've offered in this book. Unlike the utilitarian, outcomes-oriented view, the rights-oriented view does not hold business owners responsible for making a positive contribution to consumer surplus or total welfare. It allows them to use their property, according to their property rights as commonly understood, to pursue their interests as they choose, consistent with the choices of others with whom they interact, provided they do not violate any rights of those parties—even if those choices lead to suboptimal results or incidental harm to other parties.

The rights-oriented view of the market treats all participants as equals, from the individual consumer to the sole proprietor, all the way up to the national or multinational corporation. Although the scale of their influence on market outcomes is much different, they all have the right to use their resources as they choose, consistent with the rights of others to do the same. In the utilitarian, outcomes-oriented view of the market, however, consumers and business owners are treated differently. Consumers are not required to make choices between various goods and services in a way that maximizes total welfare, even though their welfare, or consumer surplus, is often considered the most important aspect of total welfare for antitrust enforcement. But business owners *are* held responsible for the maximization, or at least the promotion, of consumer surplus or total welfare, which means their rights are less valued and protected than the rights of consumers, and they are treated as merely a means to serve the ends of the economy as a whole.

MARKET POWER, MARKET FAILURE, AND COMPETITION

This imbalance between the consideration given to consumers and business owners may seem natural if firms are held to have more power in the market than consumers. This may be true in certain industries at certain times, when firms are supplying a product that is very popular or necessary, but not so when the opposite occurs, and firms fail for lack of business. As with any market interaction, the relative amount of power enjoyed by one side of the transaction ebbs and flows with economic circumstances, such as when employers have more power over terms of employment when there is high unemployment and employees have more power when there is low unemployment. It may also seem like firms have more power than consumers because firms, especially corporations, are large entities and consumers are individual (albeit "legion"). But every market transaction is between two parties, either of which can walk away if the transaction doesn't serve their interests—and if enough consumers reject a company's terms, that company can fail, no matter how large it is.

There is a specific meaning often attached to the term *market power*, however, and that meaning reflects an outcome-oriented approach to the market. As commonly understood, market power refers to a firm's ability to change a price above their cost, with a direct impact on consumer surplus and total welfare. In perfect competition, where firms must price at cost simply to stay in the market and earn normal profits, no firm has market power. As an industry becomes less competitive and firms have more latitude to raise their prices without losing all of their customers, their market power grows. Naturally, a monopoly has the most market power (although, as we saw in Chapter 2, that power is not unlimited).

Both economic and Neo-Brandeisian approaches to antitrust focus on the use (or abuse) of market power, explicitly targeting firms they believe to have it; as one casebook puts it, "the primary economic aim of competition law is to prevent the acquisition or exercise of 'market power,' as the term is used in microeconomics."[6] In addressing the autonomy of business owners, legal scholar Eleanor M. Fox makes clear that it should be protected insofar as firms lack market power, but should not be extended to those who could use it to cause harm:

> Antitrust law historically has valued freedom and autonomy of firms without market power. In contemporary debates, however, proponents seek increased autonomy for firms with leading and dominant positions in concentrated markets. Increased autonomy could mean preference for freedom of firms with power at the expense of competitive opportunity for firms without power, and possibly at the expense of lower price or greater choice for the consumer.[7]

Later she asserts that "the autonomy approach to antitrust cannot be carried to the extreme or it would trump the law. Therefore, even those who favor autonomy must make a concession to antitrust."[8] But there is nothing "extreme" about valuing and protecting the property rights of business owners when consumers have no countervailing right to "lower price or greater choice"—and this remains true for business owners who, through legitimate means, have acquired significant ability to determine their own prices. (Those who have not still have "competitive opportunity," but this is naturally limited by the actions of their competitors, as every market participant's opportunities are.)

Of course, words matter, and the use of the word "power" here is a bit insidious. It implies that this ability to raise prices represents a wrongful transfer of wealth from consumers, recalling the characterization of raising prices as "theft" that we discussed in Chapter 3. Consumers have the power to reject a price increase, seeking the products they want or need from another provider, or switching to an alternative product altogether. More generally, the term "market power" holds real-life firms up to the hypothetical ideal of perfect competition, suggesting that any price set higher than cost reflects "power" on the part of firms that is exercised wrongfully against consumers—who by implication deserve to have the only power in economic transactions, specifically the power to purchase goods and services at the lowest cost possible and therefore enjoy all the surplus generated from economic activity.

Another common term in economics that only makes sense in an outcomes-oriented view of the market system is *market failure*. This is used to describe any economic activity that leads to suboptimal welfare, such as externality (such as pollution), the exercise of "market power," or any anticompetitive behavior that is penalized by antitrust authorities. If the market fails to generate the results promised by the hypothetical state of perfect competition, the government is considered justified, if not required, to intervene and remedy the situation.[9]

Stepping back a bit, we can see that the concept of market failure begs the question of what the market is expected to do in the first place, or the purpose of the market system we discussed earlier. Naturally, if the market is expected to maximize the economic benefits to society, any failure to do so would imply a "market failure."[10] But this, once again, assumes an instrumental, outcomes-oriented view of the market process that values commercial activity only by its results. If instead we understand the market as enabling the mutually consistent pursuit of interests, it fails only if market participants are prevented from doing so. In this sense the market *cannot* fail unless it inhibits exchange—but who could do this in an economy in which the government only enforces valid rights of market participants? There is no controlling authority in the market process itself; rather, it is best considered as an emergent process from the countless transactions made in the context of legal protections provided by authorities indifferent to market outcomes.[11]

As the last phrase above indicates, thinking of the market this way is not to say it is or should be a "free-for-all." Markets exist to enable the free exercise of property rights, which requires those rights to be protected, and market participants should be prevented from engaging in fraud, deceit, or coercion—and penalized when they do so. But outside of these protections, no one should pass judgment on how property rights are exercised, what choices people make with them, or how they create economic exchange—regardless of how this exchange affects total welfare. If welfare is not assumed to be the goal of market exchange, then markets cannot "fail" to maximize it.

The outcomes-oriented view of markets also influences the way people think about competition, which has been elevated to a level of importance by antitrust advocates that it was never meant to bear. In an article that challenges the presumption that competition is unambiguously good for the economy, legal scholar Maurice Stucke sarcastically characterizes its presumed benefits as "virtues," and writes that the various approaches to antitrust enforcement, both academic and political, take them as gospel:

> Competition's virtues are so ingrained within the antitrust community that competition often takes a religious quality. The Ordoliberal, Austrian, Chicago, post-Chicago, Harvard, and Populist schools, for example, can disagree over how competition plays outs in markets, the proper antitrust goals, and the legal standards to effectuate the goals. But they unabashedly agree that competition itself is good. Antitrust policies and enforcement priorities can change with incoming administrations. But the DOJ and US Federal Trade Commission (FTC) steadfastly target horizontal restraints and erection of entry barriers via legislation. Competition authorities from around the world may disagree over substantive and procedural issues, but they all advocate competition. Indeed the labels "pro-competitive" and "anticompetitive" are synonymous with socially beneficial and detrimental conduct.[12]

But this is not the only way to think about competition. According to the rights-oriented view of the market, competition is simply the result of having multiple parties on either side of a transaction. The degree of competition has predictable effects on market outcomes, especially when the number of producers or sellers increases, which generally increases output, lowers price, and boosts consumer surplus and total welfare. Competition relies on a firm background of basic legal protections against which to operate well, but it does not depend on the law or state for its emergence. In this sense, competition is a means to the end of increasing welfare, which makes it reasonable and understandable that both economics-oriented and traditional or neo-Brandeisian antitrust advocates would promote it.

Too often, however, competition is taken to describe an end result of a process, rather than an ongoing process that happens to have beneficial effects.[13] Antitrust expert Herbert Hovenkamp writes—in quotation marks, suggesting that he recognizes it as a term of art—that "'competition' refers to a state of affairs in which prices are sufficient to cover a firm's costs, but not excessively higher, and firms are given the correct set of incentives to innovate."[14] Economic theory is partially to blame for this, with its focus on the equilibrium results of various degrees of competition in markets: perfect competition results in the lowest price and maximum welfare, monopoly results in the highest price and suboptimal welfare, and so on.

However, a true state of competition never results in a stable predictable equilibrium, like a game or match that ends, after which scores can be tallied up and winners and losers declared. Instead, the process of competition never stops—even in the case of monopoly, given that there is usually a constant threat of new rivals—and markets are always changing and evolving. An industry that seems less competitive one year may experience innovation that renders it much more competitive the next year (and vice versa). We see this especially in rapidly changing industries such as technology, in which lawsuits brought against dominant firms are made redundant before they ever reach trial. Competition properly refers to this ongoing dynamic process of firms and consumers making decisions in reaction to evolving market conditions. As such, it is always present, even when market outcomes suggest it is not, showing the category mistake of seeing competition in results rather than process, which is another aspect of an instrumental view of markets themselves.[15]

On the other hand, some supporters of antitrust take the promotion of competition too far, treating it as an end in itself to be promoted for its own sake. This is seen especially among the Neo-Brandeisians who reject the strictly economic view with its focus on consumer surplus and total welfare in favor of a more general emphasis on competition, power, and "bigness." They impute an ethical quality to competition, likening it to fairness in a game or contest. But as we discussed in Chapter 5, fairness in these contexts is not a moral issue, but rather a mechanism designed to promote the goal of the competition. To supporters of the traditional version of antitrust, competition is considered fair because it limits the concentration of power in an industry, preventing firms from becoming too large, ultimately harming consumers and smaller firms. To them, competition is not the incidental result of multiple business owners exercising their property rights in pursuit of their interests; instead, they expect to have a very particular appearance (many small firms with no power over price) and very particular results (low prices and no political influence), which antitrust authorities should be given strong powers to ensure.

In this way, traditional or Neo-Brandeisian antitrust advocates make the same mistake their more economically-focused colleagues do, targeting a vision of competition and markets that is strategically chosen to promote another goal, rather than seeing them as phenomena that emerge naturally from free choice—phenomena which also happen to produce generally good outcomes in terms of total welfare.[16] This difference has not gone unnoticed: Fox identifies the choice between "outcome orientation, on the one hand, and concern for process as well as outcome, on the other" as one of the central differences in perspectives on antitrust.[17] Most antitrust advocates, regardless of their orientation, put the cart before the horse by limiting the exercise of property rights in the name of promoting or engineering their version of competition. Even Robert Bork approvingly wrote that "antitrust was originally conceived as a limited intervention in free and private processes for the purpose of keeping those processes free. It tempered *laissez faire* in order to preserve a free market system."[18] In other words, antitrust constrains actual competition in the name of "competition," and in the end it achieves neither.

Notes

1. OVERVIEW

1. *United States v. Topcp Assocs., Inc.*, 405 U.S. 596, 610 (1972). As Alan J. Meese notes, this comparison is "a bit strange," because the "Magna Carta and the Bill of Rights, after all, place limits on the actions of governments, not individuals" ("Liberty and Antitrust in the Formative Era," *Boston University Law Review* 79(1999), 1–92, at 2).
2. *Northern Pac. Ry. Col. v. United States*, 356 U.S. 1, 4 (1958).
3. Marc Allen Eisner, *Antitrust and the Triumph of Economics: Institutions, Expertise, and Policy Change* (Chapel Hill, NC: University of North Carolina Press, 1991), 2.
4. Kenneth G. Elzinga and William Breit, *The Antitrust Penalties: A Study in Law and Economics* (New Haven, CT: Yale University Press, 1976), ix.
5. Howard M. Metzenbaum, "Address," *Antitrust Law Journal* 56(1987), 387–93, at 387.
6. Quoted in Thomas W. Hazlett, "Interview with George Stigler," *Reason*, January 1984, 44–8, at 46.
7. Eisner, *Antitrust and the Triumph of Economics*, 2
8. Andrew Shonfield, *Modern Capitalism: The Changing Balance of Public and Private Power* (London: Oxford University Press, 1965), 329.
9. See, for instance, Maurice E. Stucke, "Reconsidering Antitrust's Goals," *Boston College Law Review* 53(2012), 551–629, as well as the papers in the symposium on the goals and purpose of antitrust in *Fordham Law Review* 81:5 (2013).
10. Richard A. Posner, *Antitrust Law*, 2nd edn. (Chicago, IL: University of Chicago Press, 2001), 24.
11. Tim Wu, *The Curse of Bigness: Antitrust in the New Gilded Age* (New York: Columbia Global Reports, 2018).
12. *Ibid.*, especially chapter 2 on Brandeis; Lina M. Khan, "Amazon's Antitrust Paradox," *Yale Law Journal* 126(2017), 710–805, and "The New Brandeis

Movement: America's Antimonopoly Debate," *Journal of European Competition Law & Practice* 9(2018), 131–2. This movement has drawn substantial criticism and derision from economics-minded antitrust experts, some of whom refer to the Neo-Brandeisian approach as "hipster antitrust." For an example—and an explanation of the name itself—see Joshua D. Wright, Elyse Dorsey, Jonathan Klick, and Jan M. Rybnicek, "Requiem for a Paradox: The Dubious Rise and Inevitable Fall of Hipster Antitrust," *Arizona State Law Journal* 51(2019), 293–369.

13. Amy Klobuchar, *Antitrust: Taking on Monopoly Power from the Gilded Age to the Digital Age* (New York: Penguin, 2022).

14. See Leonard W. Weiss, "The Structure-Conduct-Performance Paradigm and Antitrust," *University of Pennsylvania Law Review* 127(1979), 1104–40. The Neo-Brandeisians argue for at least a partial return to structure-conduct-performance: see Wu, *The Curse of Bigness*, 127–39, and Khan, "Amazon's Antitrust Paradox," 744–6.

15. Robert H. Bork, *The Antitrust Paradox: A Policy at War with Itself* (New York: The Free Press, 1978). On the Chicago School of Economics in general, see Johan van Overtveldt, *The Chicago School: How the University of Chicago Assembled the Thinkers Who Revolutionized Economics and Business* (Evanston, IL: Agate, 2007), and Robert van Horn, Philip Mirowski, and Thomas A. Stapleford (eds), *Building Chicago Economics: New Perspectives on the History of America's Most Powerful Economics Program* (Cambridge: Cambridge University Press, 2011).

16. There is some dispute in academia and policymaking about whether consumer welfare or overall welfare should be the primary consideration (or, indeed, which one Bork even meant). However, because these measures are often correlated—lower prices and higher output benefit consumers directly and bring the economy overall to a higher level of efficiency and output—this debate is often seen as irrelevant (e.g., see Herbert Hovenkamp, "Implementing Antitrust's Welfare Goals," *Fordham Law Review* 81(2013), 2471–96, at Section I). For that reason, debates over the goals of antitrust tend to focus on economic welfare versus other, usually more political, considerations; that said, for an appeal to economists to adopt a more political stance to antitrust, see Mark Glick, Gabriel A. Lozada, and Darren Bush, "Why Economists Should Support Populist Antitrust Goals," *Utah Law Review* 4(2023), 769–812.

17. On the differences between the Chicago, Harvard, and post-Chicago approaches to antitrust (which are largely irrelevant to the arguments in this book), see Herbert Hovenkamp, *The Antitrust Enterprise: Principle and Execution* (Cambridge, MA: Harvard University Press, 2005), chapter 2, and William E. Kovacic, "The Intellectual DNA of Modern U.S. Competition Law for Dominant Firm Conduct: The Chicago/Harvard Double Helix," *Columbia Business Law Review* 1(2007), 1–80. (On the historical roots of

these differences, see William H. Page, "Ideological Conflict and the Origins of Antitrust Policy," *Tulane Law Review* 66(1991), 1–67.)

18. A rare exception is Rudolph Peritz, whose history of antitrust and competition law in the United States focuses on the "tensions between commitments to individual liberty and equality," stating that, in America, "the relationship between competition policy and property rights has reflected conflict coextensive with dependency since the late nineteenth century" (*Competition Policy in America 1899–1992: History, Rhetoric, Law*, Oxford: Oxford University Press, 1996, 4).

19. Posner, *Antitrust Law*, 1.

20. *Ibid.*, 2.

21. Hovenkamp, *Antitrust Enterprise*, 10.

22. Bork, *The Antitrust Paradox*, 3.

23. See, for instance, Adi Ayal's *Fairness in Antitrust: Protecting the Strong from the Weak* (Oxford: Hart, 2016), and Dominick Armentano's *Antitrust and Monopoly: Anatomy of a Policy Failure*, 2nd edn (Oakland, CA: The Independent Institute, 1990) and *Antitrust: The Case for Repeal* (Washington, DC: Cato Institute, 2001), as well as Richard Epstein's chapter "Private Property and the Public Domain: The Case of Antitrust" in J. Roland Pennock and John W. Chapman (eds), *Ethics, Economics, & the Law: NOMOS XXIV* (New York: New York University Press, 1982), 48–82. Of course, one can consider similar ethical issues and arrive at conclusions very different from mine; for example, see William J. Curran III, "Markets, Moral, or Wealth? Delusions of a Standardized Antitrust Value," *Review of Industrial Organization* 19(2001), 3–18.

24. For an overview and survey of current issues regarding the moral foundations and implications of economics, see my edited book *The Oxford Handbook of Ethics and Economics* (Oxford: Oxford University Press, 2019).

25. A possible third point is that economics is much broader than its most well-known neoclassical version, with many alternative approaches explicitly incorporating the values excluded by the mainstream. In relation to antitrust, see Ariel Ezrachi, "Sponge," *Journal of Antitrust Enforcement* 5(2017), 49–75, at 59–64.

26. See also Ayal: "The current focus in antitrust enforcement towards economically-oriented rules applied by technocratic administrative agencies avoids philosophical disputes regarding rights by focusing on scientific economic principles applied by supposedly value-neutral professionals" (*Fairness in Antitrust*, v).

2. THE ECONOMICS OF ANTITRUST

1. For a more thorough and technical explanation of what follows, see Posner, *Antitrust Law*, chapter 1; Keith Hylton, *Antitrust Law: Economic Theory and*

Common Law Evolution (Cambridge: Cambridge University Press, 2003), chapter 1; and Ayal, *Fairness in Antitrust*, chapter 2.

2. What follows is an overview of the basic welfare economics of market activity. For a philosophical look at welfare economics in general, see I. M. D. Little, *A Critique of Welfare Economics*, 2nd edn (Oxford: Oxford University Press, 1957); Amartya Sen, *Choice, Welfare and Measurement* (Cambridge, MA: Harvard University Press, 1982); and John Broome, *Weighing Goods* (Oxford: Blackwell, 1991).

3. Even if marginal costs stayed constant, little would change as long as marginal benefits fall with additional purchases.

4. Readers who are familiar with economics will recognize this as the vertical difference between the demand and supply curves at a certain level of output.

5. This simple overview neglects important factors, especially third-party effects or externalities—those will be discussed at length in Chapter 6.

6. For a seminal argument against socialist calculation, see Ludwig von Mises, *Economic Calculation in the Socialist Commonwealth* (Auburn, AL: Ludwig von Mises Institute, 1990). For a more recent reflection and extension, see Don Lavoie, *Rivalry and Central Planning: The Socialist Calculation Debate Reconsidered* (Arlington, VA: Mercatus Center, 2015).

7. Friedrich A. Hayek, "The Use of Information in Society," *American Economic Review* 35 (1945), 519–30, reprinted in *Individualism and Economic Order* (Chicago, IL: University of Chicago Press, 1948), 77–91.

8. This is usually (and ominously) called *market power*, which we'll discuss in Chapter 8.

9. This is the basis of the structure–conduct–performance paradigm's focus on industry concentration, but at this level of abstraction, it is also consistent with more theoretical approaches to industrial organization and modern antitrust.

10. For arguments supporting a consumer surplus focus, see Steven C. Salop, "Question: What Is the Real and Proper Antitrust Welfare Standard? Answer: The *True* Consumer Welfare Standard," *Loyola Consumer Law Review* 22(2010), 336–53, and Fabrizio Esposito, *The Consumer Welfare Hypothesis in Law and Economics* (Cheltenham: Elgar, 2022). Even though they oppose welfare standards in general, the Neo-Brandeisians would endorse the heightened focus on consumer well-being; on this aspect of the debate, see Herbert Hovenkamp, "Is Antitrust's Consumer Welfare Principle Imperiled?", *The Journal of Corporation Law* 45(2019), 101–130.

11. Jonathan B. Baker, "The Case for Antitrust Enforcement," *Journal of Economic Perspectives* 17:4 (2003), 27–50, at 27. The last part of the quote highlights an element I largely set aside in this book: the long-run effects of monopolization on innovation, which is a far less settled issue than the effect of anticompetitive behavior on current welfare. For more,

see Morton I. Kamien and Nancy L. Schwartz, "Market Structure and Innovation: A Survey," *Journal of Economic Literature* 13(1975), 1–37, and P. J. G. van Cayselle, "Market Structure and Innovation: A Survey of the Last Twenty Years," *De Economist* 146(1998), 391–417. (For an argument for an explicitly innovation-based approach to antitrust, see Robert D. Atkinson and David B. Audretsch, "Economic Doctrines and Approaches to Antitrust," Information Technology & Innovation Foundation, January 28, 2011; https://itif.org/publications/2011/01/28/economic-doctrines-and-approaches-antitrust/.) I need take no side in this debate, as I concede the likelihood of harm to consumers from monopolization and monopoly behavior, mainly in the present day but very possibly in the future as well.

12. For instance, see Khan, "Amazon's Antitrust Paradox," 731–6; for more on vertical merger in general, see D. Daniel Sokol, "The Transformation of Vertical Restraints: *Per Se* Illegality, the Rule of Reason, and *Per Se* Legality," *Antitrust Law Journal* 79(2014), 1003–1016.

13. For a classic treatment of resale price maintenance, see Robert H. Bork, "The Rule of Reason and the Per Se Concept: Price Fixing and Market Division," *Yale Law Journal* 75 (1966), 373–475. For recent commentary, see Benjamin Klein, "The Evolving Law and Economics of Resale Price Maintenance," *Journal of Law & Economics* 57 (2014), S161–79, as well as the articles in the first issue of volume 55 (2010) of *The Antitrust Bulletin*.

14. We shall discuss predatory pricing more in Chapter 5.

15. For more on this, which economists call contestable markets, see William J. Baumol, "Contestable Markets: An Uprising in the Theory of Industrial Structure," *American Economic Review* 72(1982), 1–15.

16. Baker, "Case for Antitrust Enforcement," 37–8.

3. THE ETHICS OF ECONOMICS

1. Raju Parakkal and Sherry Bartz-Marvez, "Capitalism, Democratic Capitalism, and the Pursuit of Antitrust Laws," *Antitrust Bulletin* 58(2013), 693–729, at 707.

2. I don't mean to suggest that economists are utilitarians at heart; many of them are unaware of this linkage, which is an artifact of the mathematization of economics in the mid-twentieth century, a technical innovation that brought it closer to utilitarianism than ever before. For more, see E. Roy Weintraub, *How Economics Became a Mathematical Science* (Durham, NC: Duke University Press, 2002).

3. Jeremy Bentham, *An Introduction to the Principles of Morals and Legislation* (London: T. Payne & Son, 1789), https://www.utilitarianism.com/jeremy-bentham/; John Stuart Mill, *Utilitarianism* (London: Parker, Son & Bourn, 1863), https://www.utilitarianism.com/mill1.htm. For an overview

and contemporary perspectives, see Ben Eggleston and Dale Miller (eds),
The Cambridge Companion to Utilitarianism (Cambridge: Cambridge
University Press, 2014).

4. These three schools of moral philosophy form the core of most introductory
ethics classes at the college level, and any "introduction to ethics" book
should flesh out the ideas.

5. Amartya Sen, "Utilitarianism and Welfarism," *Journal of Philosophy* 76(1979),
463–89.

6. Bentham, *Introduction*, chapter 1.

7. I prefer the terms *descriptive* and *prescriptive* because they sidestep to some
extent the debate about the fact/value distinction that muddies the waters
in which positive and normative bathe. In general, see Hilary Putnam,
The Collapse of the Fact/Value Dichotomy and Other Essays (Cambridge, MA:
Harvard University Press, 2004).

8. For an introduction to the debate over the self-interest assumption
in economic theory, see Amartya Sen, *On Ethics & Economics* (Oxford:
Blackwell, 1987), chapter 1.

9. This is not without its problems, such as the "impossibility theorem"
presented in Kenneth Arrow, "A Difficulty in the Concept of Social Welfare,"
Journal of Political Economy 58(1950), 328–46 and discussed widely since;
see Eric Maskin and Amartya Sen, *The Arrow Impossibility Theorem* (New
York: Columbia University Press, 2014). For more on social choice, see Sen,
Collective Choice and Social Welfare: An Expanded Edition (Cambridge, MA:
Harvard University Press, 2018).

10. The problems with GDP as a proxy of national well-being are covered in all
introductory economics textbooks; for more background, see Diane Coyle,
GDP: A Brief but Affectionate History (Princeton, NJ: Princeton University
Press, 2014).

11. For a particularly powerful assertion of this, see Louis Kaplow and Steven
Shavell, *Fairness Versus Welfare* (Cambridge, MA: Harvard University
Press, 2002). Neuroscientist Sam Harris is well-known for arguing that
utilitarianism is objectively correct; see his book *The Moral Landscape:
How Science Can Determine Human Values* (New York: Free Press, 2011).
Philosophers disagree; for one example, see Brian Earp, "Sam Harris Is
Wrong about Science and Morality," Practical Ethics: Ethics in the News
blog (University of Oxford), November 17, 2011, http://blog.practicalethics.
ox.ac.uk/2011/11/sam-harris-is-wrong-about-science-and-morality/.

12. For surveys of these problems, see J. J. C. Smart and Bernard Williams,
Utilitarianism: For and Against (Cambridge: Cambridge University Press,
1973), and Samuel Scheffler (ed.), *Consequentialism and Its Critics* (Oxford:
Oxford University Press, 1988). On the relationship between ethics and
economics, see Sen, *On Ethics & Economics*; Daniel Hausman, Michael
McPherson, and Debra Satz, *Economic Analysis, Moral Philosophy, and Public*

Policy, 3rd edn (Cambridge: Cambridge University Press, 2016); and White, *Oxford Handbook of Ethics and Economics*.

13. John Rawls, *A Theory of Justice* (Cambridge, MA: Harvard University Press, 1971), 27.

14. For a readable introduction to the debate between efficiency and equity, see Arthur Okun, *Equality and Efficiency: The Big Tradeoff* (Washington, DC: Brookings Institution Press, 1975/2015). Some question the existence of a meaningful trade-off at all: for instance, see Julian Le Grand, "Equity Versus Efficiency: The Elusive Trade-Off," *Ethics* 100(1990), 554–68.

15. Yes, I was thinking of Spock—and admit it, so were you.

16. Jules L. Coleman, "The Grounds of Welfare," *Yale Law Journal* 112(2003), 1511–43, at 1517.

17. This is not to say that Pareto improvements cannot be questioned: for example, see Hausman, McPherson, and Satz, *Economic Analysis, Moral Philosophy, and Public Policy*, 147–53; Jules L. Coleman, "Efficiency, Exchange, and Auction: Philosophic Aspects of the Economic Approach to Law," *California Law Review* 68(1980), 221–49; and Mark D. White, "Pareto, Consent, and Respect for Dignity: A Kantian Perspective," *Review of Social Economy* 67(2009), 49–70.

18. Jules L. Coleman, "Economics and the Law: A Critical Review of the Foundations of the Economic Approach to Law," *Ethics* 94: 649–79, at 662.

19. Jeremy Waldron, "Nozick and Locke: Filling the Space of Rights," *Social Philosophy and Policy* 22(2005), 81–110, at 101.

20. Ronald Dworkin, "Why Efficiency?" *Hofstra Law Review* 8(1980), 563–90, at 574.

21. Jeremy Bentham, "Nonsense Upon Stilts"—the actual title of the essay is too lengthy to print in this short volume—in *Rights, Representation, and Reform: Nonsense upon Stilts and Other Writings on the French Revolution*, (eds) Philip Schofield, Catherine Pease-Watkin, and Cyprian Blamires (Oxford: Oxford University Press, 2002), 317–401. For more on this, see Schofield, "Jeremy Bentham's 'Nonsense Upon Stilts,'" *Utilitas* 15(2003), 1–26.

22. Ronald Dworkin, "Is Wealth a Value?" *Journal of Legal Studies* 9(1980), 191–226, at 198.

23. Richard A. Posner, *The Economics of Justice*, 2nd edn (Cambridge, MA: Harvard University Press, 1983), 70. By "absolute rights" he is referring to Dworkin's conception, which I discuss next.

24. Ronald Dworkin, *Taking Rights Seriously* (Cambridge, MA: Harvard University Press, 1977), xi.

25. Deontology is covered in any introductory ethics textbook, but for more detail, see Larry Alexander and Michael Moore, "Deontological Ethics," *The Stanford Encyclopedia of Philosophy* (Winter 2021 Edition), Edward N. Zalta (ed.), https://plato.stanford.edu/archives/win2021/entries/ethics-deontological/.

26. Another example is self-defense as a legal defense to a murder charge: there is a principle against killing, but there is also one supporting self-preservation that can offset it. (The same idea extends to killing in defense of others.) Even this case is not clear-cut; see Fiona Leverick, *Killing in Self-Defence* (Oxford: Oxford University Press, 2007).

27. For more on Kant's ethics, see Roger J. Sullivan, *An Introduction to Kant's Ethics* (Cambridge: Cambridge University Press, 1994) and *Immanuel Kant's Moral Theory* (Cambridge: Cambridge University Press, 1989). On the relevance of Kantian ethics to economics, see Mark D. White, *Kantian Ethics and Economics: Autonomy, Dignity, and Character* (Stanford, CA: Stanford University Press, 2011) and "With All Due Respect: A Kantian Approach to Economics," in White, *Oxford Handbook of Ethics and Economics*, 54–76.

28. Immanuel Kant, *Grounding for the Metaphysics of Morals*, trans. James W. Ellington (Indianapolis, IN: Hackett Publishing Company, 1785/1993), 421.

29. Kant, *Grounding*, 429.

30. Anthony T. Kronman, "Wealth Maximization as a Normative Principle," *Journal of Legal Studies* 9(1980), 227–42, at 238.

31. See White, "Pareto, Consent, and Respect for Dignity."

32. Baker, "Case for Antitrust Enforcement," 27 (see also 42–6 for detail).

4.   INTRODUCING RIGHTS

1. Jamal Greene, *How Rights Went Wrong: Why Our Obsession with Rights Is Tearing America Apart* (Boston, MA: Houghton Mifflin Harcourt, 2021), xiv.

2. Dworkin, *Taking Rights Seriously*, xi.

3. Much of Dworkin's *Taking Rights Seriously* deals with precisely how to do this.

4. Ayal draws comparisons between speech rights and business rights, recommending that a balancing test be used to deal with conflicting rights in the latter as they customarily are with regard to the former, in *Fairness in Antitrust*, chapter 7. (Also, on p. 4: "The right to free trade, similarly to the right to free expression, is not without its limits—especially where actions usually protected by such a right may lead to its limitation for others for whom the system must protect as well.")

5. For an approachable history of free speech around the world, see Jacob Mchangama's *Free Speech: A History from Socrates to Social Media* (New York: Basic Books, 2022). For a succinct philosophical overview, see Nigel Warburton, *Free Speech: A Very Short Introduction* (Oxford: Oxford University Press, 2009), and for a scholarly discussion of the debates, see Len Niehoff and E. Thomas Sullivan, *Free Speech: From Core Values to Current Debates* (Cambridge: Cambridge University Press, 2022).

6. For an introduction to these debates, see Corey Brettschneider (ed.), *Religious Freedom* (New York: Penguin, 2021).

7. This distinction between principle and policy, and assigning responsibility for each to the judiciary and legislature, is due to Dworkin; see *Taking Rights Seriously*, 82–4.

8. John Stuart Mill, *On Liberty* (London: Walter Scott, 1859), 6–7 (available online at Project Gutenberg: https://www.gutenberg.org/files/34901/34901-h/34901-h.htm).

9. Even if this is allowed, it is made much more difficult, such as the process of introducing amendments to the U.S. Constitution.

10. I have to say "traditional," especially with respect to conservatives, as many on the political right in recent years have shown a willingness to interfere in the operation of private businesses, exerting political pressure to get firms to do what the government leaders want (or to stop engaging in behavior they dislike). This also explains the surprising embrace of antitrust law in recent years by *both* Democrats and Republicans (albeit for different reasons).

11. This includes, of course, the right of the government to do whatever it feels it must do to increase welfare, regardless of the effect on individual rights (which have no value outside their reflected impact on utility).

12. The conflict between Mill's liberalism and utilitarianism is much more complicated than this; for a deeper look, see John Gray, "John Stuart Mill on Liberty, Utility, and Rights," in J. Roland Pennock and John W. Chapman (eds), *Human Rights: NOMOS XXIII* (New York: New York University Press, 1981), 80–116, and David Brink, "Mill's Moral and Political Philosophy," *The Stanford Encyclopedia of Philosophy* (Fall 2022 edition), Edward N. Zalta and Uri Nodelman (eds), https://plato.stanford.edu/archives/fall2022/entries/mill-moral-political/, especially §3.11.

13. Posner, *The Economics of Justice*, 98.

14. Ayal, *Fairness in Antitrust*, 124.

15. For overviews, see F. H. Lawson and Bernard Rudden, *The Law of Property*, 3rd edn (Oxford: Oxford University Press, 2002); Gregory S. Alexander and Eduardo M. Peñalver, *An Introduction to Property Theory* (Cambridge: Cambridge University Press, 2012); and Thomas W. Merrill and Henry E. Smith, *Property (The Oxford Introductions to U.S. Law)* (Oxford: Oxford University Press, 2010). For current issues and debates, see James Penner and Henry E. Smith (eds), *Philosophical Foundations of Property Law* (Oxford: Oxford University Press, 2013).

16. For more on this distinction, see Merrill and Smith, *Property*, chapter 1, as well as their paper "What Happened to Property in Law and Economics?", *Yale Law Journal* 111(2001), 357–98, especially 360–66.

17. For example, Adi Ayal, who makes similar arguments about rights in *Fairness in Antitrust*, highlights both property rights and contract rights.

18. J. E. Penner, *The Idea of Property in Law* (Oxford: Oxford University Press, 1997), 91.

19. *Ibid.*, 91–2.
20. *Ibid.*, 80.
21. Ayal, *Fairness in Antitrust*, 125. As legal philosopher Richard Epstein writes, "if, to the economist, monopoly always raises special and urgent questions, to the common lawyer, wedded to principles of property and liberty, it is an event of supreme indifference" ("Private Property and the Public Domain", 62.
22. Ayal, *Fairness in Antitrust*, 1.
23. *Ibid.*, vi.
24. *Ibid.*, 122.
25. Epstein, "Private Property and the Public Domain," 59–60.
26. *Ibid.*, 65.
27. Dominick Armentano, *Antitrust: The Case for Repeal* (Washington, DC: Cato Institute, 2001), 69.
28. Ayal also questions the existence of consumers' rights, albeit in more detail, in *Fairness in Antitrust*, 89–101.
29. Hovenkamp, *The Antitrust Enterprise*, 1.
30. Armentano, *Antitrust: The Case for Repeal*, 69.
31. Robert H. Lande, "A Traditional and Textualist Analysis of the Goals of Antitrust: Efficiency, Preventing Theft from Consumers, and Consumer Choice," *Fordham Law Review* 81(2013), 2349–403 at 2351.
32. *Ibid.*, 2403.
33. *Ibid.*, 2357–8.
34. *Ibid.*, 2358.
35. Alex Raskolnikov, "Irredeemably Inefficient Acts: A Threat to Markets, Firms, and the Fisc," *Georgetown Law Journal* 102(2014), 1133–89, at 1151 (emphasis mine).
36. Judy Whalley, "Priorities and Practice—The Antitrust Division's Criminal Enforcement Program," *Antitrust Law Journal* 57(1988), 569–77, at 569. I thank Alan Barr for the last two references, with whom he agrees: see his article, "Do Property Rights Justify Collusive Wealth Transfers? A Commentary on White's 'Justification,'" *Antitrust Bulletin* 61(2016), 342–5.
37. For a complete history, see Charles R. Geisst, *Just Price in the Markets: A History* (New Haven, CT: Yale University Press, 2023).
38. *Adkins v. Children's Hospital*, 261 U.S. 525 (1923), at 558–9; on the Neo-Brandeisians' invocation of just price and similar ideas, see, for example, Sanjukta Paul, "Recovering the Moral Economy Foundations of the Sherman Act," *Yale Law Journal* 131(2021), 175–255.

5.   ANTITRUST VIOLATIONS AND RIGHTS

1. Alan J. Meese, "Liberty and Antitrust in the Formative Era," *Boston University Law Review* 79(1999), 1–92, at 11.

2. Phillip Areeda and Donald F. Turner, *Antitrust Law* (Boston, MA: Little, Brown & Co., 1978), 21.

3. Aristotle, *Nicomachean Ethics*, trans. David Ross (Oxford: Oxford University Press, 2009 edn), 1131a10–b15.

4. For a brief overview of fairness, see Craig L. Carr, *On Fairness* (London: Routledge, 2000/2019). In an article that argues for an approach to antitrust based on a well-defined and forceful conception of fairness, Edwin J. Hughes understands it as "a procedural concept derived from the principles of equality and autonomy. Its concerns may generally be summed up as equality," which "in the antitrust context ... finds meaning in the recognition of the rights and responsibilities of individual competitors," although the precise nature or source of those rights is left unspecified ("The Left Side of Antitrust: What Fairness Means and Why It Matters," *Marquette Law Review* 77(1994), 265–306, at 297).

5. Any microeconomics textbook should cover price discrimination, but for more detail, see Hal Varian, "Price Discrimination," in Richard Schmalensee and Robert Willig (eds), *Handbook of Industrial Organization*, Vol. 1 (North-Holland: Elsevier, 1989), 597–654 (with specific discussion of antitrust on 643–6).

6. For more on the *per se* rule and the rule of reason, see Roger D. Blair and D. Daniel Sokol, "The Rule of Reason and the Goals of Antitrust: An Economic Approach," *Antitrust Law Journal* 78(2012), 471–504, and Hylton, *Antitrust Law*, chapter 6.

7. In the United States, at the time of writing, the Department of Justice and the Federal Trade Commission were soliciting public comments on revision to their guidelines for assessing the impact of proposed mergers, which were last updated in 2010, and can be found at: https://www.justice.gov/atr/horizontal-merger-guidelines-08192010.

8. See Posner, *Antitrust Law*, chapters 7–8.

9. *Ibid.*, 40–41.

10. The seminal case of predatory pricing was *Standard Oil Co. v. United States*, 221 U.S. 1, 43 (1911), about which there is an astounding amount of controversy, starting with John S. McGee's influential skeptical take in "Predatory Pricing: The Standard Oil (N.J.) Case," *Journal of Law and Economics* 1(1958), 137–69. For more recent overviews, see the 2011 symposia marking the case's centenary in *Southern California Law Review* 85:3 and *Review of Industrial Organization* 38:3.

11. A more reliable standard is to compare the lower price to some measure of the dominant firm's costs to ascertain how much it is sacrificing its own short-term profit; for the classical presentation, which displays an admirable combination of theoretical and practical considerations, see Phillip Areeda and Donald F. Turner, "Predatory Pricing and Related Practices under Section 2 of the Sherman Act," *Harvard Law Review* 88(1975), 697–733.

12. For more details, see Posner, *Antitrust Law*, 207–23, and Hylton, *Antitrust Law*, 212–28.
13. Robert W. Crandall and Clifford Winston, "Does Antitrust Policy Improve Consumer Welfare? Assessing the Evidence," *Journal of Economic Perspectives* 17(2003), 3–26, at 3.
14. This was perhaps most famously (or infamously) defended by Milton Friedman in "The Social Responsibility of Business Is to Increase Its Profits," *New York Times* Sunday Magazine, September 13, 1970, 32. For nuanced analysis of Friedman's position, see Martin Calkins and Jonathan B. Wight, "The Ethical Lacunae in Friedman's Concept of the Manager," *Journal of Markets & Morality* 11(2008), 221–38.
15. In the same spirit, antitrust violations that are considered wrong *per se* are not wrong in a principled, deontological sense, but are simply considered to be substantially harmful often enough to be prohibited outright. These are opposed to violations that are analyzed under the rule of reason, which considers the effects on consumer surplus or welfare of a particular action or proposal. In other words, both are utilitarian in nature, but *per se* violations resemble *rule utilitarianism*, which sets general rules of actions based on their predicted effects, rather than *act utilitarianism*, which judges acts on a case-by-case basis (or according to a rule of reason).

6. HARMS AND WRONGS

1. Of course, this subsidy has to come from somewhere, usually taxation of the people who would benefit from increased positive externality. In economic terms, this is a simple transfer of funds that has no effect on total welfare itself, but encourages an increase in welfare through encouraging more efficient activity. In ethical terms, this can be seen as compensating the party who is creating the positive externality for others, which leaves the issue of whether the people being taxed for this consented to it—a common issue in this type of situation, as we saw in Chapter 3.
2. Technically, this needs only be true with respect to the last or marginal unit of output, in a way similar to our discussion of the welfare-maximizing level of output earlier.
3. Pigou's original contribution was made in his seminal work *The Economics of Welfare* (London: Macmillan, 1920), which was updated (with reference to subsequent criticisms) by William J. Baumol in "On Taxation and the Control of Externalities," *American Economic Review* 62(1972), 307–22.
4. Actually, welfare-minded economists and policymakers would not be concerned with the change in property values because it is considered a *pecuniary externality*. This type of externality involves no change in overall welfare because every dollar lost in value to the property owner represents a dollar gained to a potential buyer, merely changing the terms of the transfer

but not the total value created by it. (This is similar to the transfer effect of a change in price between consumers and sellers for a given level of output exchanged, which does not affect overall welfare.)

5. Epstein, "Private Property and the Public Domain," 61.

6. On this, see Erik Verhoef, Michiel Bliemer, Linda Steg, and Bert van Wee (eds), *Pricing in Road Transport: A Multi-Disciplinary Perspective* (Cheltenham: Elgar, 2008).

7. Of course, it all comes down to relative prices, so one could argue that drivers at other times are subsidized by virtue of not having to pay the congestion fees—again, it all comes down to your choice of status quo. Also, there is a normative aspect to subsidies, fees, and fines that is usually ignored by economists, who see them as merely costs like any other. For more on this, see Robert D. Cooter, "Prices and Sanctions," *Columbia Law Review* 84(1984), 1523–60.

8. For concise introductions to tort law, see Mark A. Geistfeld, *Tort Law: The Essentials* (Austin, TX: Wolters Kluwer, 2008) and John C. P. Goldberg and Benjamin C. Zipursky, *The Oxford Introduction to U.S. Law: Torts* (Oxford: Oxford University Press, 2010).

9. Joel Feinberg, *Harm to Others* (Oxford: Oxford University Press, 1984), 34.

10. Ernest J. Weinrib, *The Idea of Private Law* (Cambridge, MA: Harvard University Press, 2002), 352.

11. Aristotle, *Nicomachean Ethics*, 1132a (emphasis added).

12. John C. P. Goldberg and Benjamin C. Zipursky, "Torts as Wrongs," *Texas Law Review* 88(2010), 917–86, at 937.

13. Mark A. Geistfeld, "The Tort Entitlement to Physical Security as the Distributive Basis for Environmental, Health, and Safety Regulations," *Theoretical Inquiries in Law* 15(2014), 387–415, at 394.

14. Goldberg and Zipursky, "Torts as Wrongs," 937.

15. Jules L. Coleman and Arthur Ripstein, "Mischief and Misfortune," *McGill Law Journal* 41(1995), 91–131, at 116.

16. For more about these practical issues with pollution lawsuits, see Robert K. Best and James I. Collins, "Legal Issues in Pollution-Engendered Torts," *Cato Journal* 2(1982), 101–36, and Donald N. Dewees, "The Role of Tort Law in Controlling Environmental Pollution," *Canadian Public Policy* 18(1992), 425–42.

17. For more on this point, see Geistfeld, "The Tort Entitlement to Physical Security as the Distributive Basis for Environmental, Health, and Safety Regulations."

18. There is another book to be written about the ethics of the economics of crime, but suffice it to say that economists see crime in the same terms of benefit and cost as everything else. This leads some to point to the existence of "efficient crimes," such as theft in the spirit of Robin Hood,

which takes from the rich and gives to the poor, increasing overall welfare (assuming the poor value the stolen goods more than the rich do). Generally, theft is considered "inefficient" only because of the resources devoted to preventing it, not the theft itself, as well as "loss of [social value of] labour of the thief, loss of the labour of the victim who protects himself, destruction of product [lost in act of theft], and deadweight loss in underproduction of stealable goods" (Dan Usher, "Theft as a Paradigm for Departures from Efficiency," *Oxford Economic Papers* 39(1987), 235–52, at 237). In response to this general attitude, legal philosopher Jules Coleman has argued that the economic analysis of crime "has no place for the moral sentiments and virtues appropriate to matters of crime and punishment: guilt, shame, remorse, forgiveness, and mercy, to name a few. A purely economic theory of crime can only impoverish rather than enrich our understanding of the nature of crime" ("Crimes, Kickers and Transaction Structures," in J. Roland Pennock and John W. Chapman (eds), *Criminal Justice: NOMOS XXVII*, New York: New York University Press, 1985, 313–28, at 326).

19. I'm not even sure I should use "in vogue" and "tort law" in the same sentence!

20. On the economic approach to law, including both mainstream and alternative variants, see Nicholas Mercuro and Steven G. Medema, *Economics and the Law: From Posner to Post-Modernism and Beyond*, 2nd edn (Princeton, NJ: Princeton University Press, 2006).

21. George P. Fletcher, *Basic Concepts of Legal Thought* (New York: Oxford University Press, 1996), 162. It also fits very well with what the famed jurist Oliver Wendell Holmes, Jr., an influential legal realist (or pragmatist), predicted in 1897, that in terms of "the rational study of the law," "the man of the future is the man of statistics and the master of economics" ("The Path of the Law," *Harvard Law Review* 10(1897), 457–78, at 469).

22. Fletcher, *Basic Concepts of Legal Thought*, 162.

23. There are other reasons as well. In a critical review of legal writings on antitrust based on economic reasoning, Louis B. Schwartz writes that "I attribute the affinity of some fine legal minds for the imponderables of economics to the fact that economists talk the language of numbers and depict their models, however remote from the real world, in graphs whose alluring curves intersect with gratifying precision" ("On the Uses of Economics: A Review of the Antitrust Treatises," *University of Pennsylvania Law Review* 128(1979), 244–68, at 250).

24. For an overview of the economic approach to tort law, see Richard A. Posner and William M. Landes, "The Positive Economic Theory of Tort Law," *Georgia Law Review* 15(1980), 851–924, and for more detail, see Steven Shavell, *The Economic Analysis of Accident Law* (Cambridge, MA: Harvard University Press, 1987).

25. Ronald H. Coase, "The Problem of Social Cost," *Journal of Law and Economics*

3(1960), 1–44. For its attribution as the most cited legal article—and it's not even close—see Fred R. Shapiro and Michelle Pearse, "The Most-Cited Law Review Articles of All Time," *Michigan Law Review* 110(2012), 1483–520.

26. For a thorough and authoritative discussion of the Coase theorem, see Steven G. Medema, *Ronald H. Coase* (Basingstoke: Palgrave Macmillan, 1994).

27. Another Nobel laureate in economics, George Stigler, tells this story in his *Memoirs of an Unregulated Economist* (Chicago, IL: University of Chicago Press, 1988), chapter 5 ("Eureka!"). (Fun fact: Stigler also gave the Coase theorem its name.)

28. For more on misunderstandings of the Coase theorem, see Medema, *Ronald H. Coase*, 63–94.

29. Coase, "Problem of Social Cost," 3.

30. As Epstein notes, Coase's description of the problem itself identifies an injurer and a victim—the distinction is simply irrelevant to his argument ("A Theory of Strict Liability," *Journal of Legal Studies* 2(1973), 151–204, at 165). For more on Coase's rhetorical strategy, see Talcot Page, "Responsibility, Liability, and Incentive Compatibility," *Ethics* 97(1986), 240–62.

31. Richard Posner, "Strict Liability: A Comment," *Journal of Legal Studies* 2(1973), 205–21, at 216. (This was a response to Epstein's paper cited in the previous note.)

32. For more on the conception of property in the economic approach to law, see Thomas W. Merrill and Henry E. Smith, "What Happened to Property in Law and Economics?", *Yale Law Journal* 111(2001), 357–98; with reference to Coase's work in particular, see the same authors' "Making Coasean Property More Coasean," *Journal of Law and Economics* 54(2011), S77–S104.

7.   THE OBLIGATION TO MAXIMIZE WELFARE

1. Alan Moore, Dave Gibbons, and John Higgins, *Watchmen* (New York: DC Comics, 1987). For a readable philosophical treatment of Ozymandias's actions, see J. Robert Loftis, "Means, Ends, and the Critique of Pure Superheroes," in Mark D. White (ed.), *Watchmen and Philosophy: A Rorschach Test* (Hoboken, NJ: Wiley, 2009), 63–77.

2. The trolley problem was introduced by Philippa Foot in a 1967 essay included in her book *Virtues and Vices* (Oxford: Oxford University Press, 2002), chapter 2, and was further developed by Judith Jarvis Thompson in work reprinted in her book *Rights, Restitution, & Risk: Essays in Moral Theory* (Cambridge, MA: Harvard University Press, 1986), chapters 6 and 7. For later commentary, see David Edmonds, *Would You Kill the Fat Man? The Trolley Problem and What Your Answer Tells Us about Right and Wrong* (Princeton, NJ: Princeton University Press, 2013); Thomas Cathcart, *The Trolley Problem, or Would You Throw the Fat Guy Off the Bridge: A Philosophical Conundrum*

(New York: Workman, 2013); and F. M. Kamm, *The Trolley Problem Mysteries* (Oxford: Oxford University Press, 2016).

3. Ayal, *Fairness in Antitrust*, v.

4. See Mill, *On Liberty*, 103–39. (For instance, on page 117 he writes that "in proportion to the development of his individuality, each person becomes more valuable to himself, and is therefore capable of being more valuable to others.") See the references in note 12 in Chapter 4 for more on the conflict between Mill's classic liberalism and utilitarianism.

5. If you are reading this book in the distant future, ask your village elders who these people were, or substitute the musician, movie star, and athlete of your choice.

6. Mill, *On Liberty*, 180.

7. John Tomasi, "Economic Liberties and Human Rights," in Arthur M. Melzer and Steven J. Kautz (eds), *Are Markets Moral?* (Philadelphia, PA: University of Pennsylvania Press, 2018), 17–31, at 25.

8. Wu, *The Curse of Bigness*, 42.

9. *Ibid.*, 40.

10. Epstein, "Private Property and the Public Domain," 64. Tomasi also makes a strong argument that "the private economic liberties of capitalism should be recognized as basic human rights" in "Economic Liberties and Human Rights" as well as his book *Free Market Fairness* (Princeton, NJ: Princeton University Press, 2012).

11. Epstein, "Private Property and the Public Domain," 64.

12. For more on the point, in the context of various measures of well-being (including happiness), see my book *The Illusion of Well-Being: Economic Policymaking Based on Respect and Responsiveness* (London: Palgrave Macmillan, 2016).

13. This is not to dismiss offense as mere pearl-clutching; for more, see Joel Feinberg, *Offense to Others* (Oxford: Oxford University Press, 1985).

14. Wu, *The Curse of Bigness*, 91–2.

15. For an interesting investigation of similar issues with proving cause in antitrust suits, see Michael A. Carrier, "A Tort-Based Causation Framework for Antitrust Analysis," *Antitrust Law Journal* 77(2011), 401–26.

16. For more on such choices, see Lisa Tessman's two books, *Moral Failure: On the Impossible Demands of Morality* (Oxford: Oxford University Press, 2014) and *When Doing the Right Thing Is Impossible* (Oxford: Oxford University Press, 2017).

17. See Michael S. Moore, "Torture and the Balance of Evils," *Israel Law Review* 23(1989), 280–344. For a critique of threshold deontology, see Larry Alexander, "Deontology at the Threshold," *University of San Diego Law Review* 37(2000), 893–912.

18. For example, see Bob Brecher, *Torture and the Ticking Bomb* (Oxford: Blackwell, 2007), 24–31; Yvonne Ridley, *Torture: Does it Work? Interrogation*

Issues and Effectiveness in the Global War on Terror (Saffron Walden: Military Studies Press, 2016); and Jeannine Bell, "'Behind This Mortal Bone': The (In) Effectiveness of Torture," *Indiana Law Journal* 83(2008), 339–61.

19. Lee Loevinger, "Private Action—The Strongest Pillar of Antitrust," *Antitrust Bulletin* 3(1958), 167–77, at 167.

20. For an optimistic estimate, see Jonathan B. Baker, "The Case for Antitrust Enforcement," *Journal of Economic Perspectives* 17(4)(2003), 27–50, at 42–45. For a pessimistic evaluation—from the same journal issue—see Robert W. Crandall and Clifford Winston, "Does Antitrust Policy Improve Consumer Welfare? Assessing the Evidence," *Journal of Economic Perspectives* 17(4) (2003), 3–26.

21. For an examination of mergers that were predicted to have catastrophic effects on consumer surplus and welfare, see Brian C. Albrecht, Dirk Auer, Eric Fruits, and Geoffrey A. Manne, "Doomsday Mergers: A Retrospective Study of False Alarms," ICLE White Paper 2023-03-22, International Center for Law & Economics, 2023, https://laweconcenter.org/resources/doomsday-mergers-a-retrospective-study-of-false-alarms/.

22. For more on Microsoft and antitrust, see Richard B. McKensie, *Trust on Trial: How the Microsoft Case Is Reframing the Rules of Competition* (Cambridge, MA: Perseus, 2000) and Andrew I. Gavil and Harry First, *The Microsoft Antitrust Cases: Competition Policy for the Twenty-First Century* (Cambridge, MA: MIT Press, 2014).

23. Robert Pitovsky, "The Political Content of Antitrust," *University of Pennsylvania Law Review* 127(1979), 1051–75, at 1051; Wu, *The Curse of Bigness*, 55.

24. Daniel A. Crane, "Fascism and Monopoly," *Michigan Law Review* 118(2020), 1315–70, and "Antitrust as an Instrument for Democracy," *Duke Law Journal Online* 72(2022), 21–40.

25. Empirically speaking, a recent paper suggests it has little effect: Nolan McCarty and Sepehr Shahshahani, "Testing Political Antitrust," *New York University Law Review* 98(2023), in press.

26. On GDP, see Dirk Philipsen, *The Little Big Number: How GDP Came to Rule the World and What to Do about It* (Princeton, NJ: Princeton University Press, 2015), and on happiness policy, see White, *Illusion of Well-Being*.

27. See, for instance, Kenneth W. Simons, "The Crime/Tort Distinction: Legal Doctrine and Normative Perspectives," *Widener Law Journal* 17(2008), 719–32.

28. Holmes, "The Path of the Law."

29. George P. Fletcher, *Rethinking Criminal Law* (Boston, MA: Little, Brown, 1978), 408–409.

30. On the amoral consideration of penalties in the economics of crime, see Cooter, "Prices and Sanctions."

31. For an overview of the philosophy of punishment, see Thom Brooks,

Punishment: A Critical Introduction, 2nd edn (Abingdon: Routledge, 2021).

32. Again, there is an exception: *punitive damages* in civil cases, which send a clear moral signal regarding the harmful conduct. On the ambiguity inherent here, see Kenneth Mann, "Punitive Civil Sanctions: The Middleground Between Criminal and Civil Law," *Yale Law Journal* 101(1992), 1795–873.

33. Ayal, *Fairness in Antitrust*, 122. Indeed, philosopher Oliver Black defends intervention in the case of antitrust by comparing it to the worst of all crimes: "it is uncontroversial that there are circumstances in which the public interest justifies the state in infringing liberty or autonomy: think of the liberty of convicted murderers" (*Conceptual Foundations of Antitrust*, Cambridge: Cambridge University Press, 2005, 56).

34. Epstein, "Private Property and the Public Domain," 64.

35. On *mens rea*, see Paul R. Robinson, "*Mens Rea*," in Joshua Dressler (ed.), *Encyclopedia of Law & Justice*, 2nd edn (New York: Macmillan, 2002), 995–1006 (available at https://scholarship.law.upenn.edu/faculty_scholarship/34/).

36. Other effects of limited liability, as well as history of controversy over it, are noted in Paul Halpern, Michael Trebilcock, and Stuart Turnbull, "An Economic Analysis of Limited Liability in Corporation Law," *University of Toronto Law Journal* 30(1980), 117–50, and Frank H. Easterbrook and Daniel R. Fischel, "Limited Liability and the Corporation," *University of Chicago Law Review* 52(1985), 89–117.

37. Daniel Crane, "Lochnerian Antitrust," *NYU Journal of Law & Liberty* 1(2005), 496–514, at 497. Generally, Crane argues that, even in a libertarian context, antitrust is not an illegitimate exercise of state power in violation of property and contract rights if the market power addressed by antitrust arose itself "by virtue of government intervention in the market" (505).

38. *Ibid.*, 505. Directly addressing libertarian concerns, Crane writes that the "conception of liberty as freedom from government coercion is hard to reconcile with the antitrust project until one sees that the evil that antitrust addresses is caused by a governmental dislocation of the market" (512).

39. *Ibid.*, 511. Crane writes later in the same paper that, "absent the power of corporations to perpetuate their existence intergenerationally, attract capital with the promise of limited liability, and aggregate large amounts of capital in the hands of unified management, there would be little need for the antitrust laws" (512).

40. Luigi Zingales, "Friedman's Legacy: From Doctrine to Theorem," *Promarket*, October 13, 2020, https://www.promarket.org/2020/10/13/milton-friedman-legacy-doctrine-theorem/.

41. Crane, "Lochnerian Antitrust," 514.

42. Liam Murphy and Thomas Nagel, *The Myth of Ownership: Taxes and Justice* (Oxford: Oxford University Press, 2002), 8 (emphasis added).

8. RE-ENVISIONING THE MARKET

1. Marco Hafner, Martin Stepanek, Jirka Taylor, Wendy M. Troxel, and Christian van Stolk, "Why Sleep Matters—The Economic Costs of Insufficient Sleep: A Cross-Country Comparative Analysis," RAND Corporation, 2016, https://www.rand.org/content/dam/rand/pubs/research_reports/RR1700/RR1791/RAND_RR1791.pdf.

2. Jake Herway, "Need an Answer to Quiet Quitting? Start with Your Culture," Gallup Workplace, October 24, 2022, https://www.gallup.com/workplace/403598/need-answer-quiet-quitting-start-culture.aspx.

3. This myopic focus on the impact of widespread behavior on economic output is one aspect of what is called "neoliberalism," the reduction of much of everyday life to economic terms—especially in quantitative form, which is easier to manipulate or optimize according to economic models. For example, see William Davies, *The Limits of Neoliberalism: Authority, Sovereignty, and the Logic of Competition*, rev. edn (Los Angeles, CA: Sage, 2017).

4. The question of whether a person's choices should be judged by others is an issue of paternalism, which has received renewed attention in recent years due to the libertarian paternalism movement (or "nudge"); see Richard H. Thaler and Cass R. Sunstein, *Nudge: Improving Decisions about Health, Wealth, and Happiness* (New Haven, CT: Yale University Press, 2008). For arguments against libertarian paternalism, see Riccardo Rebonato, *Taking Liberties: A Critical Examination of Libertarian Paternalism* (London: Palgrave Macmillan, 2012), and Mark D. White, *The Manipulation of Choice: Ethics and Libertarian Paternalism* (London: Palgrave Macmillan, 2013).

5. Of course, a business's interests need not be solely based on profit: they can be sincerely interested in corporate social responsibility (as opposed to a strategic or opportunistic embrace), even including social goals in their founding documents (as "benefit corporations" do).

6. Andrew I. Gavil, William E. Kovacic, and Jonathan B. Baker, *Antitrust Law in Perspective: Cases, Concepts and Problems in Competition Policy*, 2nd edn (St Paul, MN: Thomson/West, 2008), 17.

7. Eleanor M. Fox, "Modernization of Antitrust: A New Equilibrium," *Cornell Law Review* 66(1981), 1140–92, at 1168.

8. Ibid.

9. This assumes that the government can improve on market outcomes, or that "government failure" will be less than "market failure." For a brief overview, see Clifford Winston, *Government Failure versus Market Failure: Microeconomic Policy Research and Government Performance* (Washington, DC: Brookings Institution Press, 2006).

10. As Herbert Hovenkamp says, "the whole purpose of antitrust is to make markets work better, and 'better' means more efficiently" (*The Antitrust Enterprise: Principle and Execution*, Cambridge, MA: Harvard University

Press, 2005, 48). Although he answers it in the second part, the first part of his statement begs the question of what it means that markets "work better," which does not necessarily imply efficiency—it could just as easily mean "in a way that coordinates and enables the mutual pursuit of interests."

11. For more on the term "market failure" itself, see Richard O. Zerbe, Jr. and Howard E. McCurdy, "The Failure of Market Failure," *Journal of Policy Analysis and Management* 18(1999), 558–78.

12. Maurice E. Stucke, "Is Competition Always Good?", *Journal of Antitrust Enforcement* 1(2013), 162–97, at 166 (footnotes omitted).

13. One can acknowledge the nature of competition as a process and value it for consequences of the process other than efficiency or welfare. For instance, Fox writes: "One overarching idea has unified these three concerns (distrust of power, concern for consumers, and commitment to opportunity for entrepreneurs): competition as process. The competition process is the preferred governor of markets. If the impersonal forces of competition, rather than public or private power, determine market behavior and outcomes, power is by definition dispersed, opportunities and incentives for firms without market power are increased, and the results are acceptable and fair" ("Modernization of Antitrust," 1154, footnotes omitted).

14. Hovenkamp, *Antitrust Enterprise*, 13.

15. The field of Austrian economics is well-known for stressing the ongoing, dynamic nature of competition; for instance, see Israel Kirzner, *Competition and Entrepreneurship* (Chicago, IL: University of Chicago Press, 1978).

16. Recall the discussion in Chapter 5 of traditional antitrust courts' focus on competitive markets as "the natural state of economic affairs."

17. Eleanor M. Fox, "Against Goals," *Fordham Law Review* 81(2013), 2157–61, at 2160.

18. Bork, *The Antitrust Paradox*, 418.

Index

Rebonato, Riccardo 157n4
religious freedom 48, 146n6
resale price maintenance 27, 143n13
reservation price 14–18
retributivist justice 93, 117
Ridley, Yvonne 154–5n18
rights 5–6, 45–62
    antitrust violations and 63–80
    business owners, of 53–7
    consumers, of 57–62
    contract 52–3, 147n17
    deontology and 38–43
    democracy and 48–9
    economic and non-economic 50,
        105–10
    externalities and 88–92
    monopolists, of 54–6
    property 50–53, 123, 147n15
    speech 39–40, 47–8, 49, 108, 146n4,
        146n5
    trumps, as 39–40, 46–50, 107–109
    utilitarianism and 38–9, 50–51
Ripstein, Arthur 94
Robinson, Paul R. 156n35
Ross, David 149n3
Rudden, Bernard 147n15
rule of law 68
rule of reason 69, 149n6
Rybnicek, Jan M. 140n12

Salop, Steven C. 142n10
Satz, Debra 144–5n12, 145n17
Scheffler, Samuel 144n12
Schmalensee, Richard 149n5
Schofield, Philip 145n21
Schwartz, Louis B. 152n23
Schwartz, Nancy 143n11
self-defense 146n26
Sen, Amartya 32, 142n2, 144n8,
    144n9, 144–5n12
Shahshahani, Sepehr 155n25
Shapiro, Fred R. 153n25
Shavell, Steven 144n11, 152n24

Sherman Act 1, 2
shrinkflation 58
Simons, Kenneth W. 155n27
Smart, J. J. C. 144n12
Smith, Henry E. 147n15, 147n16,
    153n32
social choice 144n9
social welfare function 34
socialist calculation debate 19, 142n6
Sokol, D. Daniel 143n12, 149n6
Spock, Mr 145n15
Standard Oil Co v. United States
    149n10
Stapleford, Thomas A. 140n15
Steg, Linda 151n6
Stepanek, Martin 157n1
Stigler, George 2, 153n27
structure-conduct-performance 3,
    142n9
Stucke, Maurice E. 135, 139n9
Sullivan, E. Thomas 146n5
Sullivan, Roger J. 146n27
Sunstein, Cass R. 157n4
Supreme Court (U.S.) 1, 61–2

Taylor, Jirka 157n1
Tessman, Lisa 154n16
Thaler, Richard H. 157n4
theft (price-fixing as) 60–62
third-party effects. *See* externalities
Thompson, Judith Jarvis 153n2
threshold deontology 110–14
Tomasi, John 106, 154n10
tort law 93–9, 115–19, 151n8, 152n24
torture 111–12
Trebilcock, Michael 156n36
trolley problem 102–103, 111,
    153–4n2
Troxel, Wendy M. 157n1
Turnbill, Stuart 156n36
Turner, Donald 68, 149n11
tyranny of the majority 49, 109